WOMEN AND EDUCATION
A Journey towards their Development (1880-1947)

WOMEN AND EDUCATION
A Journey towards their Development (1880-1947)

Andrey Shastri

KANISHKA PUBLISHERS, DISTRIBUTORS
NEW DELHI 110002

KANISHKA PUBLISHERS, DISTRIBUTORS
4697/5-21A, Ansari Road, Daryaganj
New Delhi -110 002
Phones : 2327 0497, 2328 8285
Fax : 011-2328 8285
E-mail : kanishka_publishing@yahoo.co.in

WOMEN AND EDUCATION:
A Journey towards their Development (1880-1947)

First Published 2021

ISBN : 978-93-89484-77-9

PRINTED IN INDIA

Published by Madan Sachdeva for Kanishka Publishers, Distributors, 4697/5-21A, Ansari Road, Daryaganj, New Delhi-110002, Typeset by Sunshine Graphics, Delhi, and Printed at Rajdhani Printers, Delhi.

Dedicated to

My Parents

Preface

'Education' has always been a debatable topic in context to women. It was a very heart-felt need to highlight the historical development of women education in United Province during pre-independence era between (1880-1947). The journey of their educational development was not an easy one. It has seen many up and downs. Several initiatives were are being made in terms of education for women. Before Independence, woman usually had the image of traditional house-wife. Acquiring higher education or even think to read or write in her life were considered as a sin. Social customs and patriarchy were not in favour to provide education to women. Since many centuries, Indian society has always been a male-dominated one. The period of pre-independence was very gloomy and dark regarding women status till the arriving of independence. The life of women were totally in the hands of their male-counter parts, who never wanted to educate their ladies. Women were taught to be good house-wife, rather than an 'educated mothers' or 'educated house-wives'. Women were subjugated under the different evils, which prevailing in the society. Women had to go through different evils like sati, female infanticide, purdah system, child marriage and many more. With the progress of time changes were make with the combined efforts of social reformers and many others intellectual persons who helped in the overall development of woman. With all these efforts a 'new woman' who able to seen in the coming of 20th century, which set up a new examples for coming generations.

Lucknow **Author**

Acknowledgement

"The dictionary is the only place that success comes before work. Work is a key to success, and hard work can help you accomplish anything."

Nothing can be done without the grace of God. So, first of all I would like to thank the 'Almighty God' for showering his blessings in my life and bestowed me with the potential power to complete my present research work.

Blessing of Guru (Teacher) is always helpful in constructing a successful pathway in one's life. So, in this regard, I would like to thank my guru, my guide Prof. S. Victor Babu of Babasaheb Bhimrao Ambedkar University, Lucknow who gave me the right direction and full support in the completion of my work. It has been my privilege to work and learn under his supervision. He has been a constructive critic, mentor and pillar of strength. All in all he has been the guiding lighthouse for my first attempt at research.

I am also grateful to all the faculty members of History Department, namely Dr. Shura Darapuri (Associate Professor, BBAU), Dr. V.M. Ravi Kumar (Assistant Professor, BBAU), Dr. Siddharth, Prof. R.B Ram for their supporting nature, and also others faculty members for their constant encouragement and support.

I also feel very much obliged to Babasaheb Bhimrao Ambedkar University (Central University), Lucknow, Uttar Pradesh, India for providing Internet facility, Computer Centre, a well equipped Digital Central Library and also a peaceful environment in which this work would have been possible.

This work became easier by the cooperation and guidance of Mrs. Meera Singh (U.P. State Archive) Lucknow, who helped me by providing valuable information. I benefitted a lot from my interaction with her. I am thankful to staff of National Archives Delhi, Nehru Memorial Library Delhi, Uttar Pradesh Archieve Lucknow, Amir-Ud-Daula Public Library Lucknow, for their valuable support in exploring sources. So, I am also greatful to them for their immense support.

In this connection, I can never forget to say thanks to all my collegues my seniors friends, Dr. Upanad, Dr. Archana, Dr. Fayaz Ahmad, Dr. Ram Prakash, Dr. Ajeet, Dr. Dharmendra Kumar, Dr. Santosh Kumar and many mores who shared their knowledge with me and also guide me in searching material related to my research, and juniors collegues Asmita, Aayushi, Shivangi, Pretty, Isha, and Arvind and also my other friends Pradeep and Aishwarya, with whom, I spent my good time during study with them, which can never be erased from my memories. I can never forget the full support of my BBAU Staff, especially Reema and Mayaram.

My family is always supportive for my study. I am always blessed by my grandfather Shri. Dhanlal, my father Dr. Pratap Narayan whose inspirational thought helped me always. My mother Mrs. Manorama, without her nurturing I could never be reach at this level. I also loved to thanks my in laws parents Dr. Rajendra Prasad and Mrs. Kiran Devi who gave their full support in acheiving my dream and also my in laws brothers. My brother Mr. Manish Deva Mathur and my little sister Ms. Beenu Shastri (research scholar Deptt. of Environmental Microbiology, BBAU) who always helped me technically. I would also like to thank my friend Mr. Atul Kumar PCS officer for helping by updating my knowlegde from different resources. I love to express my thanks to two most valuable persons in life my Daughter "Bhanvi Singh" any my little son 'Master Shivansh Singh' whose naughtiness behavior and funny activities kept me refresh always and last but not least my Husband Dr. Pankaj Kumar, whose immense love, care and full support helped me not only for this work but also for every step in my life because after marriage its really very difficult to do research work and achieve high degree like Ph.D, but he support me in every phase. I would like to pay a big gratitute to the Kanishka Publishers for his coopration and hard work, to bring this book in front of wise readers.

This book has grown out of the thesis which I submitted for the degree of Doctor of Philosophy.

At last, I am also thankful to all those who helped me directly or indirectly in this work.

–Andrey Shastri

Contents

List of Abbreviations and Glossary

Govt.	Government
NWP	Northern Western Provinces
P.S.	Primary School
S.S.	Secondary Schools
H.S.	Higher Schools
DPI	Director of Public Instruction
NWFP	North West Frontier Provinces
CP	Central Provinces
SE	Secondary Education
PE	Primary Education
HE	Higher Education
Lko.	Lucknow
UPSA	Uttar Pradesh State Archieve
NAI	National Archieve of India
NML	Nehru Memorial Library
FI	Female Infanticide
CM	Child Marriage

FE	Female Education
UP	United Provinces
No.	Number
Deptt.	Department
MEC	Methodist Episcopal Church
EIC	East India Company
IEC	Indian Education Commission
CMS	Church Missionary Society
LMS	London Missionary Society
SPG	Society for the Propogation of the Gospel
CMD	Cambridge Mission to Delhi
CM	Christian Missionaries
IT	Isabella Thoburn College of Lucknow
APM	American Presbysterian Mission
WMSP	The Women's Missionary Society of America
WFMS	Women's Foreign Missionary Society
EC	Education Commission
Zenana Teaching	Means simply a mode of instruction of females in their own houses by visiting teachers
Purdah System	Seclusion of women inside a home
Stri Dharma	Journal mainly published articles related to different women issues
Female Infanticide	The birth of a boy is an occasion for a great rejoicing; a girl causes less enthusiasm
Sati	A practice by which widows were burnt alive with the funeral pyre of their dead husbands
Thana	A police post
Pandit	A hindu priest/teacher
Maulvi	A muslim teacher
Pathshala	Elementary schools for Hindus
Makhtabs	Elementary schools for Muslims
Halkabandi Schools	Govt. primary vernacular schools

List of Tables

Maps

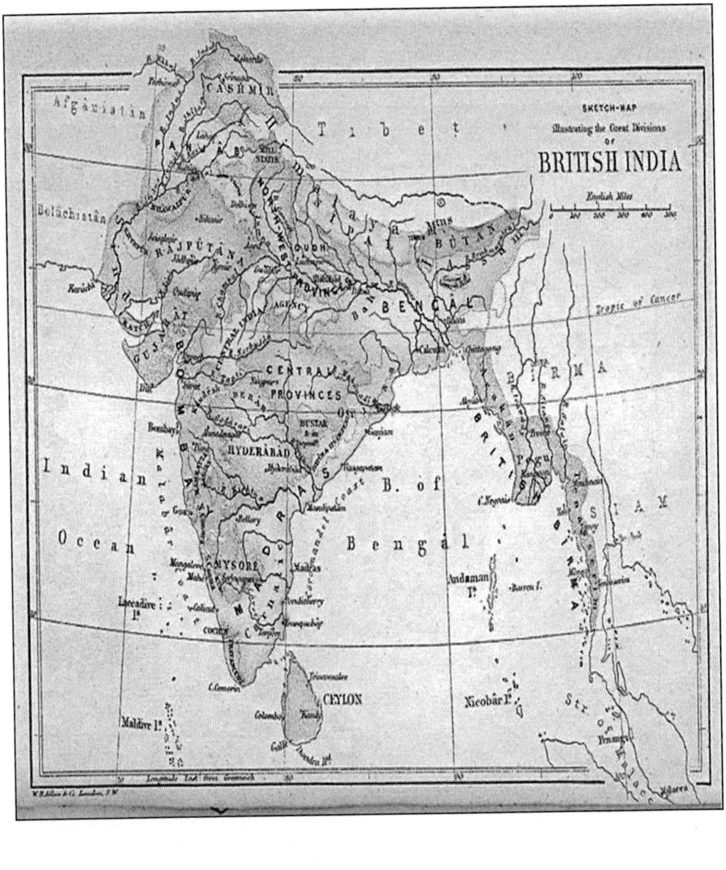
SKETCH-MAP
Illustrating the Great Divisions
OF
BRITISH INDIA
English Miles
Tibet
Afgânistân
Belûchistân
CASHMIR
RAJPUTÂNA
BENGAL
CENTRAL PROVINCES
HYDERABAD
MYSORE
BHUTAN
BURMA
SIAM
Indian
Ocean
B. of
Bengal
Tropic of Cancer
CEYLON
Andaman Iˢ.
Nicobar Iˢ.
Maldive Iˢ.
Laccadive Iˢ.
Bombay
Madras
Calcutta
Pegu
C. Comorin

OUDH
English Miles
The Terai
Himalaya Mts
Mahundi
Sitapur
Khyrabad
KHYRABAD
FYZABAD
Baraitch
R. Gogra
R. Rapti
Durriabad
LUCKNOW
LUCKNOW
Fyzabad
Oude
Tanda
Oonao
Hurdui
Sultanpur
Roy Barcilly
BAISWARA
Gonda
Pertabghar
Manickpur
Allahabad
Benares
Mirzapur
Chunar
Jounpur
R. Goomti
Ghazipur
Azimghar
Gorruckpur
R. Ganges
R. Jumna
Banda
Futtehpur
Khanpur
Kanouj
Furruckabad
Shahjehanpur
NORTH WEST PROVINCES
Longitude East from Greenwich

1

Introduction

"Literacy is a bride from misery to hope. It is a tool for daily life in modern society. It is a bulwark against poverty, and a building block of development, an essential complement to investments in roads, dams, clinics and factories. Literacy is a platforms for democratization, and a vehicle for the promotion of cultural and national identity. Especially for girls and women, it is an agent of family health and nutrition. For everyone, everywhere, literacy is, finally, the road to human progress and the means through which every man, woman and child can realize his or her full potential."

Kofi Annan

Meaning, Definition and Purpose of Education

Education is one of the certain necessity without which a man cannot live his own life. One of the great Greek philosophers Aristotle has said that man is a social animal by nature and by necessity also. The word education derived from Latin word 'e-ducere', mean "to lead out''. In a broader sense education is a process by which society deliberately transmits its whole accumulated knowledge, skills and values from one generation to another. Education is the basis for development and empowerment for every nation. In fact, it builds one's character and also plays an important role in transmitting one's culture, belief and values to others society. The development of a particular nation was measured through a well-defined system of education. Through improper education, one nation can't hardly develop. Therefore, Education is one of the most crucial factor for development. Education aims at the development of whole personality of human beings.

Men and women are the two essential organs of the society. For the progress of any civilized society or a nation, the progress of women is very important. Women are considered to be the building blocks of a family, of a society and of a nation. So, the education of women is considered to be the important tool for their development. Before we discuss women's education in United Provinces with the arrival of the British in India, let's have a glimpse of women education before colonial time. Now if we talk about the education system in Vedic age then we will find that along with the men, women also had the right to acquire education. The same kind of education was imparted to both of them without any kind of discrimination. In fact, the women were allowed to take education in Gurukul which was considered to be the most pure and pious place, in fact an education institution, "woman had free access to education and training in their learning and also free to participate in religious ceremonies and functions"[1]. "In the Vedic period among the higher section of society, the sacred initiation *(upnayan)* of girls was common and they used to go through a regular course of education as in the same manner to men. Some of them attained distinction in the arena of theology and philosophy and a considerable number of women used to follow the teaching career"[2]. Thus, from the writings of different historians it's clear that women had the right over education and can freely choose their career. Again later on with the advent of time certain changes have been made in the way towards women education. The status of women started declining from post vedic times onwards. Woman was no longer considered a person, but treated as an object having no feelings and emotions. In fact, they lost their dignity and respect during their reign. No longer attention was paid towards their educational status also. This was the time when the a slew of evils entered into the society and were the greatest obstacles in progress of women education. Women were kept under more seclusion and restriction. The Purdah system restricted them to move outside from home and not to avail any opportunity.

Later the British colonized India and started ruling. The education system which they brought was totally different from our ancient Indian education system. The initial view of this new education was merely to produce clerks for the empire[3]. Initially, the East India Company did not pay any attention towards women education. As mentioned in above line that education was brought in India only to produce some clerks in the British administration. Different schools were opened between 1825 and 1837 under the direction of the Educational committee. Earlier in 1813, when Charter Act of 1813 was made, it granted one lakh rupees in each year should be 'set apart and applied to the revival and improvement of literature and the encouragement of the learned natives of India and for the introduction and promotion of a knowledge of the science among the inhabitants of the British territories in India'[4]. Basically up to this time no clauses were made to improve the status of women education which was far lagging behind since decades.

Later on, the basic landmark in the history of education, was the Wood's Despatch of 1854, which laid down a comprehensive scheme for the whole of India in terms of education. Certain provision was made by this despatch like in Province a separate department of public instruction, the establishment of training teachers for all classes of schools, maintenance of existing government colleges, increase in the numbers of different schools and many more provisions[5]. It can be said that different clauses were made for the betterment of Indian education system. Again at primary level of education, women were still lagging behind and which was fulfilled in 1882 with the advent of Indian Education Commission. Between 1871 and 1882 remarkable progress took place and up to the pre-independence till 1947, much progress was made in terms of women education especially in primary, secondary and higher education. Different local and municipal boards also helped in maintaining education and also a lot of money was spent on Indian education through different boards and agencies.

In terms of education, the initiation was firstly made by Christian missionaries who took up the cause of female education. In fact, they understood the concept to educate the Indian women. And for this they took up the several initiatives like opening of different schools and colleges in different provinces, larger expenditure on the schools and colleges particularly to women. The early efforts of missionaries had a great impact on government to take up the issue of women education. And later on in the coming years there was a demand of English education in United Provinces and in different Provinces also. 'Missionary effort continued to play an important part in educational progress, the interest of enlightened natives was aroused, and the government accepted an increasing share of work and responsibility'[6].

Area of Research[7]

The present study will focus on Oudh region as well as in United Provinces which is now a day's called Uttar Pradesh. The area administered by the Lieutenant-Governor of Agra and Oudh lies between 23°52 and 31° 18 N and 77 ° 3 and 84 ° 39 E. The Provinces are bounded on the north by Tibet and on the north-east by Nepal; on the east and south-east by the Champaran, Saran, Shahabad and Patamau districts of Bengal; on the south by two of the Chotanagpur states in the central Provinces, Rewah and some small states in the central India agency, and Saugar district in the Central Provinces; on the west by the states of Gwalior, Dholpur and Bharatpur, the districts of Gurgaon, Delhi, Karnal and Ambala in the Punjab, and the Punjab states of Sirmur and Jubbal. The Jamuna river forms part of the western boundary, the Ganges part of the southern, and the Gandak part of the eastern; other boundaries are artificial.

According to the district surveys the areas of the two provinces are, in square miles; Agra, 83,198; Oudh, 23,966; total 107,164, including some river-beds which form district boundaries and are extruded from the district details, the total area amounts to 107,494 square miles. The area of the two native states in the provinces (Rampur and Tehri) is 5,079 square miles.

A presidency of Agra was first formed in 1834, up to which date the area then separated had been included in the Presidency of Bengal, being sometimes called the Western Provinces. In 1836 its name was changed to the Lieutenant-Governorship of the North-Western provinces. The Provinces of Oudh (Awadh is a corruption of Ajodhya, and was the name of a province before British rule) was annexed in 1856, and became a chief Commissionership with a separate administration. In 1877, the two Provinces were brought together under the Lieutenant-Governor of the North-western provinces and chief commissioner of Oudh, and in 1902 the name of the provinces was as United Province of Agra and Oudh.

The main Objectives of the research is-

- To examine the status of women education in Oudh as well as in United Provinces.
- To find out the causes of low female literacy rate in Oudh.
- To analyze the efforts of the government towards women education.
- To study briefly the efforts of missionaries regarding women education.
- To understand the views of social reformers about women education.
- To explore the different ratio of female scholars and institutions in primary education, secondary education and higher education.

Methodology and Sources

The study is based on the collection of primary sources from the Uttar Pradesh state Archieves Lucknow, National Archieves of India; New Delhi, Amir-ud-daula Public Library Lucknow, Nehru Memorial Museum and Library, Teen Murti Bhawan, New Delhi. Different government documents, proceedings, commission documents, committee proceedings, different microfilms, Indian Gazetter, District Gazetter, General Annual Administrative reports, different yearly reports of administration and Educational Administrative reports etc. have been consulted. Several secondary books and journals were also consulted in this study as to make it more better and interesting.

Chapterisation

The present work has been divided into six chapters. Basically the first chapter starts with the introduction and initially describes the status and educational condition of women before the advent of The British in India. As in Ancient India, women enjoy equal status in every domain of social life along with pursuing education also. It describes the various educational developments in the field of women education and later on diversion with the advent of the British. As it is known, education policy during their time is shaped by their needs and the ideologies of the time. The system was made often subservient to the needs and demands of the ruling classes. It can be deducted that colonial government was never serious about the education of the masses, and no attention was paid about women education.

The second chapter deals with various social evils against women. There is no doubt that social evils prevalent at that time were considered as obstacles in women education. Social evils even restricted the movement of women freely in the society. This chapter basically discuss the major social evils like Sati, Purdah system, Female Infanticide, Child Marriage or Early Marriage. These major social evils created barrier in context to women education. By practicing this women cannot move freely in the society and even did not pursue education. For example, the evil child marriage withdraws many small girls from primary education and indulge them into different household activities. So, these social evils had a negative impact on the education as well as on the social life, and status of women in the society. This chapter also shows that how Patriarchy and women education are correlated. The term 'Patriarchy' generally means that the rules and regulations of a particular society are run by the male members . So, how this Patriarchy had the positive or negative aspects on women education was also focused in this work. All these issues related to women's life were discussed.

Third chapter deals with the growth of women's education in United Provinces and also in Oudh region. It briefly explains the starting of education in India, and also what was the role of the British in education, and what kind of education they impose on Indian education system. Later on the chapter explains the major landmark in the education system like the Charter Act of 1813, Wood's Despatch 1854, the Indian Education Commission of 1882 and also various others commission related to it and also the major issue related to women education were discussed and understood briefly. Then onwards special focus was made on women education and several provisions were made for their progress and also the different problem that they faced during the receiving of education in United Provinces.

The chapters also try to explore the different stages of education like primary education, secondary education, higher education and what was the attendance of women's scholars in different institution of United Provinces since from several years.

Fourth chapter brings about the role of Christian institutions regarding female education. This chapter deals with the efforts of Christian missionaries in terms of women education. As it is well known that it was the only Christian missionaries who brought up the issue of women education in India. Later on it dragged the attention of government and social reformers to bring this issue at different arenas of different provinces. This chapter also tries to give some statistical data related to this.

Chapter five discusses the social reformers and development of women's education. This chapter tries to explore the views of some reformers who took up the cause of education (women education) like Raja Ram Mohan Roy, Lala Lajpat Rai, Annie Besant, Sarojini Naidu and also others more reformers of global level and also describes the different intellectuals and highly official educated persons who shared their views in the favor of women education in United Provinces. In context of women education or women rights the name of Savitribai Jyotirao Phule cannot be forgotten. No doubt she played an important role in improving women's rights in India during British period. She worked very hard to abolish discrimination system which flourish in India and also unfair treatment of people based on caste and gender. She is regarded as one of the most important icon of the social reform in India, who scarified her life for improving the women status in Indian society.

Last sixth chapter conclusion mainly describes the whole summary of the work in brief and draws some findings of the research.

FOOTNOTES

1. N.L. Gupta, Women Education through The Ages, Concept Publishing Company, New Delhi, 2000., p. 19.
2. Ibid.
3. Krishna Kumar, Politics of Education in Colonial India, Second Edition, Sage Publication, New Delhi, 2005., p.13.

4. The Imperial Gazetteer of India, The Indian Empire, Vol. IV Administrative, Oxford, 1907.
5. Ibid, p.413.
6. The Imperial Gazetteer of India, The Indian Empire, Vol. IV, Oxford, 1907.
7. The Imperial Gazetteer of India, Vol. XXIV, Oxford, 1908.

2

Review of Literature

The review of literature holds an important part in any research as it helps in determining the scope of research and to study the selected problem in a better way. Therefore, the current study is an effort to put research in the right direction. For the present study, different review has been carried out.

Mary Carpenter paper on, Female Education in India (1868) starts her writing by saying that, 'India is said to be the brightest jewel in the British Crown'. The author very keenly describes the social condition of women in India as well as the educational condition. Mary very keenly wrote that missionaries were very dedicated and also shown their interest in the education of women in India. The different missionary ladies formed different associations for the education of the women in the east, and slowly in different parts also. She very minutely describes the social condition of Indian women through masculine lens and wrote that the male counters of our country were very jealous from the success of our Indian wives and daughters and that's why they never support them in any kind of educational activities. She further wrote that the women of India are treated like slaves.

M.S. Sundaram's paper on Education in British India (1964) discuss the whole view of education in British India and also on one hand discussed the merits and demerits of Indian education. Author also took the Gokhale's recommendation about free universal compulsory free education. He also took the problems of establishing universal education. He also discussed about the various stages of education. Author also discussed about the plans and prospects of education for the future.

Lalita Panigrahi book entitled, Female Infanticide and British Social Policy, first published in June 1972, basically depicts the traditional Hindu society of the nineteenth century. The western ideas, culture and humanism had impacted Indian society. The book discuss the worst social evils, namely female infanticide which was highly prevalent at that time in Indian society especially in United Provinces of that time (present Uttar Pradesh) and which was suppressed by the enforcement of social legislation spreading over nearly a century. Author made special focus on the different complexities of the problems of social legislation and social reforms in India.

Y.B. Mathur book entitled Women's Education in India 1813-1966, published in 1973, is a landmark to through light on women's education in India. It shows the changing status of women education during the early decades of the nineteenth century. The author also talks about the various social customs, practices like purdah, sati, child marriage and also different prejudices which were creating hurdles against education of women.

Another book of Aparna Basu entitled, The Growth and Political Development in India; 1898-1920, published in 1974, discuss some aspects of the educational problems in India between the period of 1898 to 1920. Author also discussed the impact of modern education on Indian society. However, she believes that new education system produced a class of people, who later led the national movement; but at the same time, they received a limited vision by this education.

Aparna Basu's another book entitled, The History of Indian Education (1982), deals with the several issues like the origin of the Indian Educational system, the indigenous system, technical education, comparative colonial policies, and also the education of civil servants.

Kumkum Sangari and Sudesh Vaid edited book, Recasting Women-Essays in Colonial History, 1989, briefly describes the social status of women. The essays in this collection either attempt to construct the lived culture or social relations of a particular life and place through available records, or to show the making of a selective tradition through discursive and political processes. The essay in this book mainly discuss the dominant nature of Hindu community, largely of North India and also deals with the middle class. The authors try to show the changing status of women. The book basically tries to examine the impact of patriarchy on women's daily lives during the colonial period, specifically in relation to caste and class.

S.P. Agarwal and J.C. Agarwal book entitled, Women's Education in India, 1992, gives a brief analysis of women's education in India. The book is divided in to 4 parts. First part deals with the historical review, present status and perspective plan. In historical review, it mainly describes the women's education through the ages and also the writings of modern thinkers. Second part mainly talks about the different statistical indicators of Pre-independence India and after Independence. Part III mainly deals with the scholarly writings in Indian educational journals and newspapers since independence and Part IV has some selected bibliographies on women's education and allied topics.

N.L. Gupta book entitled, Women Education Through The Ages, 2000, mainly focuses on women education through various phases of Indian history like Vedic period, post-vedic period, Jain-Buddhist system, Muslim rule, British rule and in the post-independence era. Authors also focus on the various factors and phenomenon responsible for bolting or opening the doors of education for women, this has also been critically analyzed by the author. This book provides the brief history of women education from ancient times till modern time and also describes major policies by the government or NGO's at present.

Gauri Srivastava's book entitled, Women's Higher Education in the 19th century, 2000, emphasized on the status of women's education in the 19th and 20th century in western India. The author argues that 19th century can be called as "age of women" for all over the world for their rights and wrongs. She also discussed how feminist consciousness began to spread in Europe after French revolution and by the end of century feminist ideas were being expressed by radicals in England, France and Germany. The book also throws light on the history of women education in India during 19th and 20th century and what efforts were made by the Christian missionaries, social reformers and also by the British government.

Suresh Chandra Ghosh's book entitled, Birth of A New India, 2001, is a good work to understand the contributions of mainly three British reformers namely Bentick, Dalhousie and Curzon in the nineteenth century for the benefit of the Indian society. Bentick, Dalhousie and Curzon reforms tried to make India modern with their reforms which no doubt were beneficial for the Indian people. Curzon thus made an indirect contribution through his reforms by making Indian University Act. Bentick contributed in growing British administration by making English language as official language. Dalhousie's governorship saw the crystallization of the educational experiments carried out by him. One great contribution made by the Bentick and Dalhousie to improve the lot of the Indian society by stripping off the various existing social evils like sati, infanticide, child marriage and polygamy. Later on writer shows that it was Dalhousie being Governor-General support officially to female education in India as "no single change in the habits of the people" was likely to lead more important and beneficial consequences than the introduction of education for their female children". It can be said that the contribution of Bentick, Dalhousie and Curzon for making new India remained largely unknown.

Sabyasachi Bhattacharya edited book entitled, The Development of Women's Education in India: A Collection of Documents 1800-1920, published in 2001, is a collection of complete documents on women education in India. This book deals with the historical pattern of development of women's education in India. Author mainly begins around the middle of the nineteenth century when the institutional structure of the education system as it was in the twentieth century, began to take shape. This collection includes a great deal on statistical information on women education not only in United Provinces but also in different parts of India. This documented book gives brief estimates on different issues related to women for example–no. of girls schools in British India, no. of girls enrolled in primary, secondary and higher education in different provinces in different years, and total expenditure on female education in different colleges in Provinces. So it's a great effort by the author for the researcher to get knowledge on the status of Indian women on education and also the different issues which create hurdle in women education.

Sabyasachi Bhattacharya edited book entitled Education and the Disprivileged: Nineteenth and Twentieth Century India (2002), discussed the familiar issue of unequal access to education in a new perspective. There is a gap between the privileged and dis-privileged section of society. It also provides historical perspective to understand the major loop holes in the educational opportunities of the marginalized sections of society like tribals, dalits, women and backward classes. The book provides a broad area of education and the dis-privileged, side by side it also gives a rich source of empirical evidence on educational growth among the dis-privileged during colonial period.

Jane Martin and Joyce Goodman book entitled Women and Education, 1800-1980, (2004) is a beautiful collection of data on British women educators, feminists and leaders in the period of 1800-1980. The author was motivated by the absence of women in orthodox accounts of British education generally as well as the exemplar of feminists revisionism. While writing this study author starting point was a joint interest in the culture and social relationships that underlay the struggles to gain greater access for women to the public world of education. This book mainly deals with the stories of six women's whose participation in the politics of education is little known like: Elizabeth Hamilton (1785-1816), Sarah Austin (1793-1867), Jane Agnes Chessar (1835-80), Mary Dendy (1855-1933), Shena D. Simon (1883-1980), and Margaret Cole (1893-1980). The primary goal of the author is to re-map the understandings of women's participation in changing philosophy, policy and practice in education.

S. Shabbir's book entitled History of Educational Development in Vidharbha From 1882 to1932 A.D (2005), is a creation of the historical development of education in Vidharbha from 1882 to 1932 A.D. the author also identifies that change in the education pattern from indigenous nature to modern perspective at all levels. The book also shows that how education works as an instrument for social changes in the region. It also refers over-all educational backwardness of females, low caste and aboriginals tribes with a growing assertion of claims to social and political recognition. It also highlights that how sustainable development was possible in Vidharbha only through educational expansion.

Hayden J A Bellenoit book entitled Missionary Education and Empire in Late Colonial India,1860-1920 (2007 published), completely gives knowledge on education of India during 19th century and 20th century, also contribution of missionaries in United Province and also about the social condition of India during 19th and 20th century. Author says that 'Education was, politically and imperially-speaking, crucial for the British during the generation of Macualy and after to fill the lower tiers of a rapidly spawning-out colonial bureaucracy'. Education which was given to Indian was just to fulfill the clerks jobs, which was only filled by the Indians. Later on author also says that 'apart from its political and imperial realities, education was also, more important, a formative social and intellectual factor in the emergences of modern India'.

Indrani Sen's work, Memsahib's Writings-Colonial Narrative on Indian Women (2008), reprint in 2015, briefly described the diversity of white women's writings. She describes that white women of colonial India wrote extensively and how they maintained their journals, diaries, letters, novels, and how they penned their memories, over the period between 19th century. The books also draws a wide variety of women's diaries, letters, memories, travel-narratives, missionary tracts, medical writings, housekeeping journals, sociological studies, novels and short stories. The book brings the historical perspective on certain issues like purdah system, female infanticide, female education and many more.

Women Education and Development, a book written by Dr. Manilei Serto (2011), says that no nation can achieve success unless education is accorded to all its citizens. Author argues that how women or girls education is important in today's life scenario as it was in older times. It's very important subject and importance should be paid toward it. The book also dealt with several topics like– education in India, Literacy in India, Women in India and importance of education, the educational change, some ideals in the education of women, changing status of women, educational system and society, the educational machinery, the elective system and college curriculum, social activities and hygienic education, women and society, domestic environment of college women, women's rights and female education, national policy for the empowerment of women. Undoubtedly this book relate us with the several issues related to women in past and present time.

In the work, A Student's History of India: 1800-1737 (1945), 2011 J P Naik and Sayed Nurullah have clearly brought the major objective of the colonial and post–colonial education system and its development. The author clearly discussed every critical stage in educational development in colonial period, as well as it also explained the rise of each important decision and the consequences thereof. The book first talks about Charter Act of 1813 to 1973. It also discussed about the role of Christian missionaries in India. They act as a catalyst of modern education.

Geraldine Forbes book entitled Women in Modern India (1998) 2012, is a systematic and comprehensive study of Indian Women of 19th and 20th century of both colonial and post-colonial India. She starts with the reform movements, which was established by men to educate women and demonstrates that how education changed their lives and enabled them to take part in public life. She also documents the formation of different organization related to their different issues, their participation in the struggle for freedom, their role in the colonial economy, and the development of women's movement in India since 1947. The author also explain that with the efforts of some Indian reformers, the British took initiative for reforms like sati, child marriage, widowhood, polygamy and prohibition on education which became an important issues related to women.

Another book by the author V. Geetha entitled Gender, very significantly describes the word 'Gender'. Author clearly shows that gender is everywhere and also explain the meaning of gender in terms of female and male. They both are having different attributes and roles. Several themes were discussed in this book. Geetha suggests significantly that gender ' is both part of the world we live in, as well as a way of understanding the world'.

R C Mishra's book entitled Women Education, 2013, explains education as a fundamental human right for girls and women and also a development necessity. The author describes how there is a large gender disparities in enrolment. The book also shows that throughout all over the world, education is regarded as the key factor in overcoming the different barrier that women had faced and education also acts as a basic tool for empowering women and bringing them into the main path of development. Education not only provides basic knowledge and different skills how to improve health and livelihood but it also empowers women to take their rightful decision in the development process as well as in society. This book covers all the issues related to women's education.

Education in Colonial India: Historical Insights (2013), a book edited by Deepak Kumar and others, deals with the debates and development of education in colonial India. The book shows the transmission of knowledge through different agents and institutions of education in modern India from a historical perspective. This volume traces the growth of knowledge in India in modern times and its conflict with the existing societal and religious expectation and also of the conflict between individual and institutional views.

Suresh Chandra Ghosh in his work entitled The History of Education in Modern: 1752-2012 (2013), deals with the history of education in colonial and post-colonial India. It examines crucial issues that shaped India's education system viz., introduction of English education, the Despatch of 1854, the genesis of Curzon's university reforms of 1899-1905 and educational policy of post-Independence India. The author also discusses that how the Indian Universities Act of 1904 enacted by the viceroy Curzon intended to introduce radical changes in the functioning of the five existing Universities in Calcutta, Bombay, Madras, Lahore and Allahabad. He also discussed about the recommendation made by the National Knowledge Commission, the Yaspal Committee report on the functioning of bodies in higher and technical education. The author has also elucidated the Right to Education Act (RTE) which, according to him, is one of the most extraordinary reforms in elementary education since independence.

Krishna Kumar's Politics of Education in Colonial India (2014) is a significant contribution of the histography of the colonial education in India. Parimala V. Rao edited book entitled New Perspective in the History of Indian Education (2014), basically deals with the old and new perspective of education. According to the author the 'old perspective' in the history of Indian education can be divided in to four categories namely: imperialist, anti-imperialist, post modern and nationalist. On the same hand 'new perspective' arises due to two important drawbacks in the old perspectives; namely factual errors and a complete silencing of the voice of the truly opposed one's. Another reason for the growth of new perspective in this volume is the complete absence of the poor, women, untouchables and mainly lower caste which was mainly disappear in the old perspective. In this volume one chapter on 'Dalit Initiatives in Education' written by Eleanor Zelliot mainly describes the records of tribals and tribulations faced by the early reformers from different caste. Another essay by Radha Gayatri on 'Silent Voices' shows how educated Indian women's perceptions about themselves and critically examines their roles within Indian society.

V. Geetha book Patriarchy (2015), clearly describes the origin and meaning of patriarchy. Author says that Patriarchy means the 'absolute rule of the father or the eldest male member over his family'. Author also shows how Patriarchy is supported by Kinship structure, relationships of production and the caste system. Very clearly and in a concise manner through this book, author helps us to understand the complexity of Patriarchy and also the way we live.

Minna Galbraith book entitled The Education of the Women of India: Primary source Edition (1912), is a good work by author and briefly described about the Education of women in India. The book also describes the different statistics of different provinces in India. The whole information about women education was provided through this book, regarding the importance of education in Vedic lives and in modern lives and author also took the other different issues like purdah, sati and so on which creates hurdle's in women's life. The book also provides some government report and some quinnenial report of certain years related to women education.

3

Social Evils against Women

History of women reveals that women always occupied a subordinate position and also enjoyed very limited freedom in this patriarchal society. Women's status in the society as compared to men was always secondary. The traditional paternalistic attitude of men towards women was almost negligible. The attitude towards women did not bring about transformation in the practical aspects of their life. Education develops one's character and personality also. The education was never considered as an important issue for women.

Women constitute nearly half of the population from our total population. Lagging behind the half population uneducated not even a country could grow. Even in the ancient time women enjoyed a equal status in the society. And had equal rights over everything, even they are supposed to acquire higher education. Later on the status of women started declining and different evils crept into the society. Purdah system, child marriage, sati system, jauhar system, devadasi system, cruelty of female infanticide, female foeticide and many more evils emerged in the society which were against women. As a result, less attention was paid towards this dimension.

By the coming of 19th century, the position of Indian women in society had declined and most of the girls from respectable families were denied from literacy[1]. For the growth of every society and every nation education is the most important tool of empowerment. As education was denied to women in 19th century, they remained totally ignorant about it. Educational opportunities were very rare in the case of girls, as they are more subjected towards different household duties which was the nature of patriarchal Indian society. The patriliенal structure was there not only in United Provinces, but in fact in all over India. It was considered a great obstacles in achieving education.

Patriarchy is a very well-known term in context of Indian society. As in the Indian sub-continent, the term implies 'male domination', 'male prejudice (against women)' or simply in other words 'male power'[2]. The word 'patriarchy' is likely to figure frequently catches all words to describe the diverse ills that women suffer from so many decades. Put simply, it can be described as 'the absolute rule of the male members or eldest male member over his family members especially women'. Basically, patriarchy is thus the rule by the father in the family. In a patriarchal society women have to struggle for their own right, for education, for property right and also to choose their partners in marriages. V. Geetha defines the provisional definition of patriarchy and refine it as:

> Patriarchy, rests on defined notions of masculine and feminine, is hold in place by sexual and property arrangements that privileges men's choices, desire and interests over and above those of the women in their lives and is sustained by social relationships and cultural practices which celebrate heterosexuality, female fertility and motherhood on the one hand and valorize female subordination to masculine authority and virility on the other.[3]

The above lines V. Geetha rightly captures the ground realities of Indian society. As Indian society is also patriarchal, this system did not favour education to women. The men did not support their women to move into higher education not only in United Provinces but also in other provinces. The status of women education in United Provinces was already in very backward condition as compared to other provinces like Bombay, Bengal and others presidencies. Above all this, there were different reasons for the backwardness of female education in United Provinces like child marriage, early widowhood of girls, poverty, purdah system, insufficient trained female teachers and inspectresses, lack of proper fund, and last but not least the patriarchal nature of our society. This was one of the evils which stops women to move forward in their life. As woman were considered as recipients of male patronage. 'The early 19th century public discourse on reform thus not only had limited impact on society as a whole, it also signified the patriarchal control of the educated Indians males over the private sphere or domestic arena reserved for women'.[4] As men had a full control over the women rights and life. They can't even take a single decision on their own about her life. So, it seems that the patriarchy had its strong roots in the Indian society and even on the women life.

Traditionally, according to patriarchy the role of women was simply as a housewife or mother, child marriage and immediate post-pubertal consummation of marriage, early and frequent child bearing, and finally, secluded widowhood. According to this definition there was no space and meaning of education for girls in their life. They were completely devoid of it. Although it was provided up to a very early age as to have very basic knowledge as well as they should have knowledge just to read and write her name. At that time it was very rudimentary, informal and major focus was on the religious education, which usually help them to fulfill their domestic roles perfectly. At this time the education especially for women has the purpose of training women so that they will be good wives, as well as good mothers in the house. This is the only meaning of education for women by the patriarchal nature, which they usually decided for women. The purpose of education and the quality of education which was giving to them it only indicated as to get better management of the household activities. 'No major structural changes in patriarchy occurred through this type of education, and thus 'female education' proved to be the least difficult segment of social reform[5]. Basically, the patriarchal system became very powerful during this period and it began to restrict the activities of women, as they are the mere puppets at the hands of men. The majority of women were looked down upon in the society and can't march forward ahead in the life towards higher development. This kind of attitude or belief adversely affected the position of Indian women. Her position in the family as well as in society became very low. It aroused a picture of women of having very weak personality. Unfortunately, patriarchal system along with other socio-historical factors resulted in the subordination of women in Indian society.

Next evil which was the most prevailing in colonial India that was 'Sati'. It was the most cruel evil practiced ever attempted into the mirror of Indian society. It is interesting to note that women status became the main focus of the colonial state as well as of the Indians educated people.[6] Everybody including colonialists, Indians educated, higher officers, the British and even social reformers were in favor of removing these cruel evils, which degraded the women's status in the society and also one of the great obstacles towards the progress of women education. 'It was the focus of intense scrutiny from various colonial observers, for whom it became one of the India's most iconic and controversial spectacles, the social and political significance of which far exceeded its actual occurrence. As quoted by R. Hurst (British Police Officer) in 1929 in Charu Gupta's work, 'Sati must be one of those things that look quite different from different viewpoints. If we cannot see it from the orthodox Hindu's side, we cannot know what aspect it shows to him. Nor can we expect to persuade him that our view of it is clearer or truer than this.[7]

Social evils was one of the subjects which was taken up the British, missionaries and also by different social reformers. There was more focus on Sati, but attention was also paid towards female infanticide, child marriage, polygamy system, the oppression of Hindu widows, female illiteracy and mainly purdah system, which was targeted by every educated people. Before the British took up the reins of India, they expressed their horror towards the cruelties like sati both as spectators or observers. The imposition of inhuman practices and several restrictions like burning of widows, widowhood at an early age, child marriage and absolute illiteracy of Indian women are some of the practices by which men still maintained their supremacy in society. All these evils proved to be great obstacles in obtaining education for women.

In the early decades of the 19th century Sati continued to be one of the major social issue for female and male social reformers. It was one of the main cruel gendered social practices through which the Indian women were suffering. The issue of Sati as a one of the 'social reform' was undoubtedly one of the complicated ones, and women of all provinces were suffering from this cruel evil. Literally, Sati means 'virtuous woman' and it it commonly denoted any woman who usually burnt alive on her husband's funeral pyre. In the colonial period the British extended the term, in its anglicised form 'suttee', to the rite itself, with the result that sati is now used for both the practice and the practitioners. Usually the custom of Sati mainly practiced in Hindu cultural context. If a woman accumulates enough sat (goodness) through her devotion towards her husband she can become sati, usually, though not exclusively, by following him onto the pyre.[8] Sati was one of the major issues through which Indian women were suffering. In fact, long before the coming of the British, Sati was a part of the cultural set up of India. The issue of Sati was a question of discussion for various imperialist and nationalist and its 'abolition' became a touchstone for colonial social reform. Custom of Sati was so deep rooted in our Hindu culture that its abolition was mainly discarded by some orthodox Hindu people. As a result Sati was increasingly simplistically explained as arising out of the Indian woman's two supposedly essential characteristics–her inherent religiosity and her extreme devotion to her husband.[9] In the work, Memsahib's Writing's by Indrani Sen it is quoted there by Mrs. E. J. Chapman, who primarily outlines the role of the colonial government in fighting Sati and in passing anti-Sati legislation in 1829. The issue of Sati as social reform was one of the most complicated issue. The most striking point was that, she makes no mention of Indian reform leaders like Raja Ram Mohan Roy who fought this battle. Indeed, it is remarkable how these women's writings maintain a silence on the role of Indian reformers who actively participated in each of the major struggle (viz. Raja Ram Mohan Roy's campaign against Sati and Ishwar Chandra Vidhyasagar's struggles to legalize widow remarriage).[10]

Sati became a cause celebre, both in India and at home, and was debated not only by the Govt. of India, but also by the East India Company, Board of Directors, and its proprietors and stockholders, the British Parliament, missionaries, philanthropists and the regional and national press.[11] Sati was one of the horror issues which was suppressed by everybody, which really degraded the status of women in India. It is one of the most sensational and emotional issue. This type of 'sensational' subjects reached up to large numbers of audience than even before, as accounts of these atrocities were distilled down into pamphlets and cheap tracts that could be disturbed among different poorer section of the Indian community. Despite the fact that women were marginalized in the entire debate on Sati, a discussion on this issue from male participants both (indigenous and foreign) shows an unusual enthusiasm in the issues related to women.

Official debate was also going in the East India Company (EIC), in govt. circles, and lot of campaign was done by different missionary groups and also by several educated Indian people in different provinces, as it was the most shocking aspects of Indian women about their life and also which could attract the public attention. Basically, all social customs denied women access to education. They were usually imagined as belonging to this private world. Different reformers of the 19th century mainly concerned about the lower status of women in the society and among them Vidyasagar, one of the famous Sanskritist and educationalist of the 19th century, emerged as a champion of widow-remarriage and of female education. In the context of different customs he stated, 'Women are comparatively weak and due to the tyranny of social customs subordinated to men. Owing to this weakness and domination by men, women have to spend their lives in ignominy and subordination. The dominant male tyrannize over, and exploit them as they like, and women have to submit to the same and eke out their existence.[12] Above lines interpret that women were considered as an object who really were fighting for their identity in those days and the decision of their life was totally in the hands of their male counter parts. The reformers, educated people, revivalists and progressive section of people, was much more concerned with the status of women and were instrumental in beginning a movement directed towards changing the status of the women.

Superficially, Sati appears to be one of the 'abhorrent' practices that nationalist leaders and social reformers who sought to eliminate it from our Indian culture. The abolition of Sati by the British Officer William Bentick, and Indian reformers like Raja Ram Mohan Roy, Dwarkanath Tagore in 1829 has created a great moment in the history of women in modern India. Initially, there was some orthodox opposition to this move, orchestrated through the hastily established Dharma Sabha[13], in 20th century as most accepted the prohibition of Sati as fact. This is not to suggest, however, that the rite was universally censured; both 'reformist' and 'revivalist' treatments of sati throughout this period remained doubtful. Many nationalist leaders and different social reformers actually criticize the practice. Many social reformers and several nationalists criticize this practice. Even M.K Gandhi stated that he found 'nothing praiseworthy' in it and even approved the British for outlawing it.[14] This cruel practice done in context of women seems very horrible and they did not have access to education and also there were no liberty for women.

Many social evils were prevalent in the society which restricted the overall development of the women in Indian culture. And among many social evils, Purdah was more problematic issue among women no matter what category women belong. Seclusion inside a home, no matter how large and luxurious, had caused women to liken their condition to that of birds in a cage having with no choice in life[15]. All these evils in the form of social custom left woman like a bird which has no wings to fly and can't do anything of her own choice. Moreover, from the late 19th century, onwards, the issue of purdah system became one of the interesting subject, as passionately discussed, and had a very divergent views, especially from very ancient time the removal of purdah had been identified as one of the items on the social reforms agenda. Apart from the efforts of male social reformers it was also discussed in the female writings by the works of Indrani Sen.

Considerable discussion was going on whether Purdah system was prevalent in ancient India or not? as in ancient times the women had access towards education as compared to boys. So, it pretends that this system may be less prevalent at that time. The presence of ladies in social and public gathering was a normal feature in the Vedic times.[16] Again A.S. Altekar says that, 'it would however appear that soon after the beginning of the Christian Era, a section of society began to advocate a greater seclusion or a kind of restriction for women. This was more particularly in the case of most of the royal families, where this notion began to prevail that royal ladies should not come within the public gaze[17]. It may have been prevailing in few of the royal families of Hindus, but their number was very small. Purdah system basically hampers girls education as they can't move freely in the society, also can't take active participation in any of educational activities.

Even the problem of Purdah was the major issue in the progress of women's education in Oudh region. As less no. of girls attended the schools, as a result, most of the schools were closed down in the city. The people of the house were in favour of zenana teaching, as to study at home. Purdah system was the main reason for the backwardness of women because of it majority of the girls had very less attendance in Lucknow schools and in many others parts of United Provinces. As the Director of the north-west makes vigorous observation that, the North-West Provinces and Oudh have made far less progress in female education than any other part of India. Among girls of school-age in these Provinces not more than one out of 217 is at school. The average for the whole of India being one in 50. Reasons were defined as:

1. To excessive indifference on the part of the people.
2. To powerful customs,
3. The less facilities that were provided to them,

And many more reasons were there for the less education of women in United Provinces. It is somewhere true that the people generally are not in favor of educating the girl child, and may even be hostile to it in some classes and places, but it is difficult to say whether this feeling is stronger or more widespread here than in any other Province.[18]

Actually here girls were less educated and left uneducated as there is not any kind of desire of educating them. Many of them drop-out at an very early age, as less attention was paid towards their school management and education. However, social customs stand in the way of girls education. It is one of the great barrier in terms of their education. Basically, these customs are not confined in United Provinces also but there was a nature of revolt in all over India. The major obstacle is purdah system in women life. In Plains, purdah is said to be strictly enforced among muslims and the higher castes of Hindus at 9 yrs of age or earlier, girls being usually married at 8 or

9 yrs of age. In the Etawah District, purdah system is so strictly observed among the middle classes in the towns. A girl even age of 8 is seldom allowed out of the house. Same in the Bulandshahr board, girls belonging to respectable families cannot appear in public after 6 or 7 yrs[19]. So these examples were showing the condition of women in the society. In short, these social customs belonging cuts girls education at an very early age. As they remain away from the elementary education.

Later on with the rapid advancement in time and on intellectual level, there is a distinct desire of educating the womenfolk. But the desire is subject to a lot of qualifications and the time has not come when these limits which parents wish to impose on the education of girls could be exceeded without harming the cause of female education. Till now, no scene of female education can have any chance of success if it does not conform to the inherent conservation of the ancient families of Oudh who are hopelessly purdah-ridden. In Oudh, the purdah was strongly followed, that even the most highly educated men of the zamindari families in Oudh are not ready to give it up. Even if few ladies who want to give it off they are treated more or less as out-caste.

It is believed that the Purdah, in spite of its evils, is a greater boon than female education minus Purdah and the purdah must be kept up at all cost. It is also believed that it is quite unnecessary to give higher education to women which would enable them to read their religious books and fit them for their duties as mothers and housewives. They are quite restricted or narrow sense of the term, provided the purdah was not threatened.[20] Although from the above statement, it's clear that in Oudh region there is a restricted desire of female education. As it was not given so much of importance as compared to boys. Main reason behind this was that the male counterparts of the family were least interested in female education.

They don't want to see them as a educated person, but they just only know how to read and write their name and should have basic knowledge about household activities. There is a desire of good mothers, good wives rather than an educated lady. As a result, very less progress was made in girl schools of Oudh. Purdah system is the first and foremost cause towards women education in Oudh. Even the public has almost fully recognized its importance's in terms of girls 'education.' It requires a great deal of patience and persuasion on the part of the public spiritual few to convince the masses that the educationalist progress of a community depends materially on the education of women'.[21] Women education is very low in this province as compared to Bombay and Bengal. Purdah system was considered as a stumbling block in the way of women education. Greatest hindrances came in the cause of female education is different types of religious prejudices. In addition, there is a great demand regarding the abolition of purdah system as it denied women from their basic right of education as well as with this they can't move freely in this society and also can't pursue higher education in their life. It would seems that women now want mobility and choice in their life, and demands to abolish this system and really wants to go ahead in life. As compared to other Provinces women were not doing anything as in other Provinces they do. It cannot be denied, therefore, that the purdah is detrimental to women education. 'the members of the Indian women's organization attacked purdah as inhibiting female education. Moreover, they urged the government to provide schools for girls where strict purdah could be maintained (by sending covered carriages to pick up the girls, providing covered entrances, surrounding the schools with high walls, and vigorously excluding males from the grounds), to provide purdah hospitals and to set up purdah parks. They did not accept purdah, nor did they think it could be easily abolished[22].

The general adoption of the Purdah System by some royal families of Hindu community is more less a subsequent to the advent of the Muslim rule. It was an additional protection for the women folk by strangers. Generally, Hindus spoke about the ' Golden Age' when women moved freely in the society. ' the abuses of the system were regarded as the result of "custom", further explained by some as an imitation of Muslim or Hindu court customs, or as practices adopted basically to protect women during the Muslim invasion[23]. Even today it is in practice and practiced a lot in a well-educated civilized society. Even, Hindu feminists began to see purdah as a custom brought to India by Muslim invaders and a cause of women's fall from the high position as they hold in ancient time which was popularly known as "Golden Age". 'What had been the feminists issue of the 19th century had, by the third decade of the 20th century, became an issue which divided Hindu feminists, with their insistences on a particular interpretation of the "Golden Age", from Muslim feminists, who had grown protective of their religion. While discussion of purdah caused a rift between advocates of women's right, the custom itself was never vigorously attacked'.[24]

The status and the position of Indian women, always been a very controversial subject. The position of women in any society reflects the image of women of a particular country. In a country like India, women always been treated as a 'Devi' or 'Goddess'; the perfect guide or guru of her children. And on the same hand, she has always been criticized for the weakness of her character. As from the various Hindu literature sources, it is quite clear that Indian women never enjoyed a free and independent status, and their rights in the society were considerably restricted. Certainly different social evils played a very vital role in shaping the destiny of Indian women. At that time, they had full rights over every thing. And even in marital situation. Child marriage or early marriage is one of the stumbling blocks in terms of girls' education. As it drop-out the majority of girls very beginning from schools at an very early age. In the Vedic age, women used to be well-educated in any subject, well cultivated and were refined in their manners as well as in etiquettes. Apart from this, women of Vedic age imparted training in spiritual and different temporal subjects. As well as at the time women used to take part in decision-making bodies of the society. Same in terms of marriage considerable freedom seemed to be given to the girls and boys for selecting a perfect match for them. The meaning of marriage was very pious for girls and boys ss child marriage was not very much prevalent in Vedic times. Actually there was a tradition of imparting knowledge to both girl and boy.

Later on with the passage of time many ups and downs came into the woman life and their status started declining. Many new practices emerged in the Indian society. Child marriage or early marriage was one of the most prevalent evil that was going on in all provinces. As girls education begins at the age of 5 and ends at 12 or 13.[25] Due to child marriage many small age girls were withdrawn from schools. Generally, educational progress of a community depends materially on the education of women. Child marriage is one of the stumbling blocks in the progress of women education in United Provinces which is the most backward provinces in terms of female education. As Pandit Tara Datt Gairola, the member of Legislative Council of United Provinces also said that 'the question of female education in India bristle with difficulties of various kinds; the social customs of the people, such as early marriage of girls, purdah system, caste prejudices etc., are some of the drawbacks against a universal diffusion of knowledge among the women of India[26]. Child marriage was forced to put down by different male reformers, female reformer, also by different educated people as it had many drastic consequences of women life especially on her education and secondly on their health, and another consequences of child marriage that it lead to early women widowhood. As early widowhood of women completely withdraws her from educational life and engrossed them into different household activities.

Paradoxical though it may appear, it seems that the Sati custom, which became fairly popular at that time, helped the cause of early marriage to some extent.[27] Altekar also holds the view that joint family system prevailing in society was somehow favorable for early marriages in India. Still, the society knows about the consequences of child marriage, i.e., there was the danger of early widowhood of a newly small age girl. But such a calamity was believed to be a decree of fate, which could not be set at nought by any human effort. During the colonial time, usually 8 or 9 yrs was considered as a marriageable age of Indian girls. 'With the introduction of western ideas and civilization the educated sections of society began to feel the necessity of deferring marriages to a more advanced age. Different social conferences began to advocate the cause of post-puberty marriage during the nineties of the last century, but their efforts were not appreciably successful till the beginning of the 20th century[28].

In 1929, the child marriage restraint act was passed by prescribing the minimum age of boys and girls, and it came into force on 1st April, 1930.

The Provisions of the Act of 1929 were:

1. The Child Marriage Restraint Act prescribed the minimum age of marriage for boys and girls at 18 and 14, respectively.

2. It brings down the penal provisions for the different persons like male adults who marry young girls i.e., girls under the age of 14, the persons who perform child marriage etc.
3. It also provides punishment for the offence which may be fine or imprisonment.[29]

The Census Report for India of 1931 gave the following figures of the number of girls who are married under the age of 15 by age groups:

Age group	**Percentage married**
0 to1	0.8
1 to 2	1.2
2 to 3	2.0
3 to 4	4.2
4 to 5	6.6
5 to 10	19.3
10 to 15	38.1

Thus, nearly one girl in 100 girls of less than one year of age is married and the same horrible fact is repeated in all the other age group under 15. One consequences of this is the almost unbelievable number of child widows in the country. The figures of widows as follows:

Age group	**Actual number of widows**
0 to 1	1515
1 to 2	1785
2 to 3	3485
3 to 4	9076
4 to 5	15019
5 to 11	105482
10 to 15	185339

Source: Hansa Mehta (IInd Inst.) Printed material-3, All India Women Conference, Anti-child Marriage Committee, Bulletin No. 1, Child marriage: The extent of the evil.

From the Census of 1931, it is clear that the percentage of married girls and number of widows are increasing at the age of 15. The child marriage, and its consequences restrict a woman to pursue education in her life, as it was a stumbling block in the progress of women in her life. The degree of freedom given to women in a society and to take part in public life gives a good idea about the nature of its administration and somehow it enables us to know about the progress of women. The history of the position and status of women in any society or of any country is very interesting and debatable topic. In fact, they were given the status of goddess by the society. Woman or even a single girl child was treated like a "Lakshmi" by the family. But all these statements seems to be bookish languages as very less practiced in this society where these different cruel custom were taking place in context of female. Generally, in all patriarchal societies the birth of a girl was generally treated as unwelcome event by the family, whereas on the same hand the birth of a boy was equally treated as an event of joy by the family. Almost everywhere the son was valued more than the daughter. He was treated as a permanent economic asset of the family. The daughter, on the other hand was treated as a burden for the family. Different historical evidences show that in India the daughter was not welcome. 'Some thinkers have even pointed out that a talented and well behaved daughter may be better than a son. In cultured circles such a daughter was regarded as the pride of the family.[30] In fact, woman of the ancient times or of Vedic age was more intelligent and intellectual in terms of education, imparting training of any kind etc. Several times they proved to be much more better than man. Basically, there are no references of this evil custom in the Vedic, epic or classical literature. A.S. Altekar opined that, if female infanticide had at all been practiced, it must have been confined to a very small section of society.

The practice of Infanticide has prevailed amongst many countries of the world at some stage of their civilization or another. The forms which it took, and the motives which led to the crime varied as much from provinces to provinces with circumstances as with the habits and character of the people amongst whom it was found to exist.[31] Female infanticide was mainly confined to infants who were either poisoned or put to death by various means, at birth itself. The practice of female infanticide in India did not arise from any kind of superstitious motives, in fact it was a practice which arose out of the social institutions and customs of the people.

As mentioned earlier that this evil was not prevalent in Vedic period, later on with the passage of time with the advent of different dynasties the condition of women becomes very deplorable. As Lalita Panigrahi observed that, 'there is no satisfactory evidence to prove that female infanticide originated with the Muhammad invasions. As emperor Jahangir also issued a proclamation prohibiting female infanticide. The crime was also condemned by Guru Gobind Singh. In fact, it is quite probable that the practice spread more widely when the Mughal govt. disintegrated in the 18th century. The anarchic conditions destroyed the security of life and property of India. These conditions made the security of woman's dignity extremely difficult[32]. This evil took most cruel form in this period because women lost their rights over different things. However, they had no choice for marriage of their own will. Hence, less attention was paid towards them and also on their education. The result was that they were considered as a burden to the family and for parents also. It seems that female infanticide or foeticide became more prevalent from the 18th century and still continued even today in modern times not very frequently but somewhere among rural areas or in among less educated families.

Female infanticide also continued in the 19th century in many of the different communities of colonial India as known from very widely available various archival documentation. The intentional killing of girl-child because of the low value religious and economic-associated of daughter as compared to son or in other words it can be said that, the undesirable want of female child instead of a male child which automatically lead to the killing of female infants is termed as female infanticide. Though, infanticide was theologically condemned by many of the religious scriptures like dharmshastras, dharmsutras and also like Puranas, yet no references were found regarding infanticide like cruel evil. As it also continued to be suppressed by different religions, the idea that women were subjugated to men since beginning is one of the most absurd notions that have come down to us from the period of the enlightenment of the 18th century. Woman occupied not only a free but also a highly respected position among all savages and all barbarians of the lower and middle stages and partly even of the upper stages. It is beyond any possibility of existence of female infanticide during the period before replacement of mother right with that of father right.[33]

The female infanticide took more cruel shape as to inherit a right in father's property. This was considered to be one of the reasons which forwarded this practice. As Manu quoted that, eldest son of the family has the full right to inherit the property right in father's property. At the same time daughters were deprived of her share in father's property. The religious and economic futility of daughters, it appears in course of time, made her a liability enough to be killed by her own family members at the time of her birth itself. This cruel evil as killing of daughters continued throughout the pre-colonial period, as it remains continued, even after the enactment of Anti-infanticide Act of 1870 passed during British colonialism.

Earlier the government of the North-Western provinces were not in a position to follow very vigorous policy as towards the suppression of female infanticide in NWP, as it was very deep rooted in Indian society. But later on great effort was taken by the Governor-General like Auckland and Dalhousie and even by the Lt. Governor of the NWP, especially James Thomason and John Colvin.[34] The Governor-General, Lord Auckland, was scarcely satisfied with the policy of direct interference with regard to the registration of births of newly born girl babies. As he was assured by the Commissioner in 1840, that the system of registration appears to do well in the district Jaunpur. It is stated that 'in the past 6 months, 30 girls had been preserved and by 1843 there were 246 girls in Jaunpur and 157 in Azamgarh'[35]. It can be said that the practice was slow, but still the progress was going on. It boosted the feeling towards the suppression of this crime. The success of the plans pursued in the different districts of NWP system, actually depended on the personal influence of the Magistrates and on the exertions of the local officers.

In 1845, the Tehsildar reported the preservation of 284 girls amongst the Bais Rajputs of Azamgarh; however in 1855 the total number of girls was only 89[36]. In Agra provinces also different preventive measures were introduced by the government in 1854. According to George Camphell, the then magistrate of Azamgarh in

1854, is in view that nothing could be affected without the supervision of the police. He also said that nothing could be achieved only by making different kinds of effective speeches. He rightly said that rank had its price and the buying and selling of ranks as of everything else must be regulated by demand and supply and not by sumptuary laws, also in view that unequal marriages, almost led the girl's father to pay a heavy dowry, were the major causes of the crime.[37] Several types of preventive measures were taken by different highest officers of different districts of United Provinces, not much of the success could be attained but efforts were going on. As sometime the success of the movement also depended much on the personal interest taken by the individual officers also.

Like in Allahabad, in Bara pargana, right from the very beginning different decisive and coercive measures introduced in 1841 by Robert Montgomery, the then magistrate of the district, where he found no effect on infanticidal races.[38] As for this they involved a strict supervision by four important members of the village namely the chaprasi (peon), gorait (messenger), chowkidar (watchman) and mid wife, each one of them acting as a check on another.[39] All these different people were appointed as to report the birth of a girl in the suspected clans at the thana[40], so that an eye must be kept on the criminal by looking forward the birth of a newly born girl. If they failed in giving proper report then they were subjected towards a heavy penalty. With this so much of effective and tight security in the year 1842, there were 28 girls alive. It can be said that little progress was made in this direction, in very careful manner. Even though there was a steady increase in the number of girls and later on in coming year in 1850, there were 83. Female infanticide was practiced in different districts of United provinces like in Mainpuri or in Allahabad, Azamgarh and in many more districts.

In pre-colonial India there was no established rule of law against killing of girl child. Later on there was a growth in the ideas of liberation among individuals and with the growth of English or western education among Indian citizens it led into the modern values of equality and liberty in the society, which further led into the different social and political movements. Basically it gives a symbol of eradication of the tradition and different social customs like Sati immolation, beginning of widow remarriage, ban on child marriage and also prohibition of female infanticide etc. Later on, in spite of the Female Infanticide Act of 1870, passed by the government as to suppress the practice. Act also recommended to punish the criminals along with the punishment like sentence to death, also like the transportation of life. Keeping in view towards this crime certain number of articles were written towards the opposition of this crime. As one of the newspaper, the Urdu Akhbar wrote, The Infanticide act of 1870 has not been able to suppress infanticide, but on the contrary, has tended to make the crime assume a worst aspect. Formerly girls were killed at the very moment of their birth, but now, since the Infanticide Act has come in force, they are allowed to perish from sickness before they attain to the age of a year or two. It will thus be at once perceived that the old practice was less abominable than the present one.[41] The custom was very prevalent in other provinces also apart from North-Western provinces. It can be said that custom of female infanticide was not uniformly followed throughout the castes, but although it remained prevalent in certain castes, as killing of daughters were in active phase.

The custom of female infanticide continued throughout the 19th century not only in the Purihar community of Rajputs of Hamirpur district in particular but also in many communities throughout India. In fact, in 19th century it was believed that India was the only country on the Earth where custom like female infanticide was known to exist.[42] There is an article on Infanticide views, "It took its rise in the time of Hindu Rajahs and Rajpoot princes, and that in that age it was not regarded as a crime. The general custom was to kill them as soon as they were born by stuffing cow dung in to their mouths. This incidence was quite horrible. As in some cases they were killed by plunging their faces in milk; while in others, they were ruthlessly strangled with a strong chord. Different types of incidences were very horrible in case of female infanticide. For eg. In case of Punjab province, this custom was prevalent among a particular tribe after murdering girls at their birth, to place a piece of Gur (Jaggery) in their mouth, and a roll of cotton in their hand, and repeat the words, feed on the gur, and spin the cotton. Come in to the world no more, but send brothers."[43]

All these references shows that it is an atrocious (horrifying) evil, which continues to be practiced by different castes and tribes of NWP. This type of wicked evil really needed a strong check by the Police and by the government. To stop this evil was not a question in NWP and other provinces also where small infants were brutally killed or murdered by different methods. In any tribe or among any clans, if the boys and girls among them were counted in small proportion of the latter to the former would clearly prove the existence of this cruel practice. Government was very slow in this process and yet not done anything effective in this manner. As quoted by one of the Vernacular newspaper that heavy expenditure in the marriages of Hindu daughters considered to be the chief cause of the evil in question. Later on the writer urges that the government should prohibit extravagant marriage expenses and adopt the following measures in order to check this evil:

1. The chief lambardar in every village in which there are any suspected families should keep a register in which he should enter the name of each woman who belongs to any of those families as soon as she become pregnant. The tahsildar or the naib-tahsildar should inspect the register once a month.
2. Each midwife should be required to execute a bond to the effect that she will not procure an abortion and that she will report the name of every woman as soon as she becomes pregnant, to the lambardar.
3. No girl who is born dead or has died soon after her birth should be allowed to be buried until a post-mortem examination has been made.
4. All weak and sick girls should be sent by the lambardar to the doctor for treatment. If the cause of the weakness or sickness of any girl is found to be that she has not been well fed by her mother, the latter should be punished.[44]

All these points which are highly urged by the writer to the government, shows that if there will be keen strictness among the different peoples of the villages then only there can be a stop towards this evil. As mentioned earlier that this evil somewhere led by the heavy expenditure in the marriages of Hindu woman. Due to the heavy demands from the boys family automatically led the girls to commit suicide as to get rid from this issue, as well the girls family did not want their next child to be a daughter, as all these circumstances led to the process of female infanticide in different parts of India. In the NWP the abuse was very prevalent in Mynpoory, till Mr. C. Raikes, the collector and magistrate, directed his attention to it. In the district of Etawah it is still prevalent, and the Delhi Gazetteer of the 3rd June asserts that the Rajpoot tribes there indulge in the practice. Mr. Moore, the magistrate, has fixed the crime upon them, and solicited the orders of the supreme government for enforcing the law in the district. The govt. NWP is heartily bent on removing the abuse and has laid down the rules for achieving that end.[45] On the basis of above evidence it can be said that the crime was prevalent among the Rajputs tribes of NWP, and in different clans also. In spite of the Act on prohibition of female infanticide, the crime was prevalent in many of the districts of the NWP. In the year of 1887, in some of the districts like Agra, Mainpuri, Etawah, Etah, Fatehgarh, Badaun and Bareilly where there is excessive mortality of female children in the year after birth. In the district like Meerut, there is excessive female infant mortality. On the other hand in Aligarh, there is existence of infanticide of female infants. On the other hand districts like Cawnpore, Allahabad, Jaunpur, Azamgarh, Mirzapur, Gazipur, Ballia, in all these districts there is preponderance of male births[46]. All the information shows that in majority of the districts there is excessive female mortality rate than male. Table 2.1 given below shows the percentage of boys and girls as well as percentage of death infants male and female in the various districts of NWP in the year of 1888.

Table 2.1

Percentage showing no. of births of boys and girls and percentages of deaths among boys infant and girls infants in NWP.

District	Percentage of births of boys	Percentage of births of girls	Percentage of deaths of male infants	Percentage of deaths of female infants
English rates	50.68	49.32	17.24	14.27
Saharanpur	54.66	45.34	20.46	20.59
Muzaffarnagar	47.89	52.11	20.8	25

(Contd...)

Meerut	54.48	45.52	12.5	20.4
Bulanshahr	52.18	47.82	21.93	23.94
Aligarh	57.82	42.18	21.17	11.29
Agra	53.54	46.46	13.7	22.03
Fatehgarh	48.38	51.62	17.15	21.96
Mainpuri	53.88	46.12	20.07	31.48
Etawah	48.29	51.71	28.28	23.58
Etah	52.75	47.25	22.6	32.03
Bijnor	53.79	46.21	23.78	25.64
Moradabad	48.14	51.86	26.92	35.71
Budaun	50	50	29.88	42.4
Bareilly	50.39	49.61	29.68	39.68
Shahjahanpur	60	40	33.33	31.25
Cawnpore	53.68	46.32	20.58	18.18
Fatehpur	43.59	56.05	20	15.68
Allahabad	60	40	26.66	20
Hamirpur	49.09	50.91	22.22	23.21
Jaunpur	61.11	38.89	15.15	15.47
Basti	48.51	51.49	26.93	20
Azamgarh	57.08	48.92	19.77	18.23
Mirzapur	7368	26.32	28.57	20
Ghazipur	57.54	42.46	11.47	13.33
Ballia	57.14	42.86	18.75	16.66
Jalaun	51.21	48.79	16.07	15.62
Jhansi	56.25	43.75	33.33	14.28

Source: File 708 of 1888, Annual Report on Female infanticide in the NWP for year ending 31st March 1887, Police Deptt., NWP and Oudh.

Table 2.1 clearly shows that there is a variation of percentage of births of boys and females in the different districts of NWP. As for the district like Fatehgarh, Etawah, Moradabad, Fatehpur there are greater percentage of births of girls and lower the percentage of deaths of female small babies. As it also indicate that there was less indication of female infanticide in the above mentioned district. By and large, it can be said that the percentage of boys birth was higher in every districts of NWP as compared to girls birth rate. In between many decades as on the concept of female mortality different reasons were given like sometime the small pox, plague, malaria etc. were the reasons for the great excess of female deaths in different provinces.

The Infanticide Act of 1870 did not have very fast result, as it was not strictly enforced in the different provinces. In some of the years in some districts it was exempted as no source of female infanticide was found in different provinces. As on '1st April 1895 the Act was in force in 567 villages in 20 districts in NWP and Oudh provinces. The opening population was 86692 of which 7211 were boys and 5122 girls under the age of six. During the year two villages in the Fatehgarh and five in the Jaunpur district were exempted[47]. The figures mentioned above clearly shows that still there is large number of boys as compared to girls. Although still, in many of the district's the repressive action of the law appeared still to be needed in Bareilly, Shahjahanpur and in the district like Cawnpore also. On the other hand in the year of 1895-96 the Infanticide crime was recognized in the different district like Fatehpur, Jaunpur, Gazipur, Ballia, Basti. The statistics which are available are too small to draw any conclusion, but one thing was confirmed that in spite of the Act of 1870, the crime was prevalent, although in small figures also. The district reports, showed that the working of the Act received very varying degrees of attention in the several districts. Later on in the year of 1897-98 the Act was in force in 500 villages, and the largest number, 155 being in the Mainpuri district[48]. In between the year nearly about 85 villages were exempted from the operations of the Act, leaving behind 415 villages where the Act was still in force, containing the population of 59937. Districts like Fatehpur, Jaunpur and Ballia were completely exempted from the Act. The table 2.2 clearly shows the number of birth and deaths of boys and girls in the year of 1897 and resultant population on 1st April 1898.

Table 2.2

Increment in girls population

	Boys	**Girls**
Population under six 1st April 1898	5206	3706
Births	1394	1247
Deaths	693	686
Arrivals	636	512
Removals	693	653
Transfers to population over six	994	542
Resultant population,	4856	3584

Source: Administration report of 1897-98, NWP and Oudh

Table 2.2 shows the improvement as can be observed in the context of girls under the age of 6, as well as the percentage of girls population to total population as rising from 41.58 in 1896 to 42.96 in 1897. As this shows that there is a slight increase in girls population.

Table 2.3

Shows the ratio of births and deaths of female in the proclaimed population as compared with the provincial figures.

% of births of girls to total births	Provincial rates for NWP and Oudh for 1897	Average rate for 1897-98, for the proclaimed population
	47.85	47.22
% of deaths of girls under one year to total deaths under one year	48.64	48.56
% of death of girls under one year to total girl births	29.62	25.58

Source: Administrative report of NWP and Oudh, 1897-98.

Table 2.3 gives a comparative look of births and deaths of female infants in the proclaimed population as compared with the provincial statistics. The death rate of infant female population in the proclaimed villages is actually lower, as compared on the whole than the provincial death rate. Actually, these statistics indicate that female infanticide is there but very little practiced. Or in the other hands, the returns of the year are satisfactory. As mentioned earlier that the districts which noted earlier as being especially open to the suspicion for practicing female infanticide are Mainpuri, Etawah and Fatehgarh, and in Mainpuri special efforts were made to improve the administration of the Act.

Table 2.4

The following figures shows the results for the year, 1899-1900.

	Boys	Girls
Population under Six on 1st April 1899	3406	2217
Births	1149	980
Deaths	449	432
Arrivals	416	415
Removals	473	381
Transfers to population over 6	656	401
Resultant population on 1st April 1900	3393	2398

Source: Administrative report of NWP and Oudh, 1899-1900.

The initial population differs from the resultant population shown in the previous report in consequences of the omission of the villages which were exempted during the year. The basic average ratio of births as between boys and girls in infanticide districts was 54 boys to 46 girls, the corresponding provincial rates for 1899 being 52 and 48. The average death rate of children under one year in infanticide districts was 52.34 boys to 47.66 girls. As the proportion of boys to 100 girls was, at the commencement of the year, 153 and at it's close to 148.[49] Still some of the districts found guilty by practicing female infanticide while some of the districts were exempted from the Act. But even from the different statistics it is clear that the birth rate of boys is higher than female. Somewhere the figures are too small to draw any conclusion and somewhere the results are unfavourable.

Later on in 1925, Govt. of United Provinces when desired of making special provision in the Indian Penal Code to deal with the cases of infanticides, the Govt. of India enclosed a copy of a letter, as dated 25 July, 1925, from the Govt. of Bombay and its enclosures on the subject. It referred the law on the question then in force in England and also in many countries. It also mentioned the debate in the House of Lords in 1922 when the Infanticide Act of that year was under consideration. Lord Loreburn proposed, "...to leave it to the judge and not to the jury to determine whether the mater should be manslaughter or murder". Lord Alverstone opined that, ".... To leave the law as it stood and simply to provide that a judge might record the sentence of death instead of pronouncing it in open court". Another person, Lord James Hereford proposed, corresponding to those of the Child Murder (trial) Bill, which was passed in 1922, "where a woman was charged with the murder of her infant child and evidence was given that at the time the offence was committed, the woman had not fully recovered from the effect of giving birth to the child. The jury was to be empowered to convict her of manslaughter instead of murder".[50]

Basically, the relevant provisions of the Act contained in the first two sub-sections of Section I are as follows:

(1) Where a woman by any willful act or omission causes the death of her newly born child, but at the times of the act or omission she had not fully recovered from the effect of

giving birth to such child, and by reason there of the balance of her mind then disturbed, she shall, not withstanding that the circumstances were such that but for this Act the offence would have amounted to murder, be guilty, to wit, of infanticide, and may for such offence be dealt with and punished as if she had been guilty of the offence of manslaughter of such child.

(2) Where upon the trial of a woman for the murder of her newly-born child, the jury are of opinion that she by any willful Act or omission caused its death, but that at the time of the Act or omission she had not fully recovered from the effect of giving birth to such child, and that by reason there of the balance of her mind was then disturbed, the jury may, not withstanding that the circumstances were such that but for the provisions of this Act they might have returned a verdict of murder, return in lieu there of a verdict of infanticide.[51]"

As the different provisions of the Bill as mentioned above, provided that the mother may be punished if she had been found guilty of the offence of manslaughter, in which case the punishment was under section 5 of the offences against the Person Act of 1861, at the discretion of the court and may be up to a maximum of penal servitude for life. Lord Birkenhead is of the views that, "the mere fact that the woman had not recovered from effect of childbirth should not be sufficient but that it should also be necessary that the emotional and physical strain should have so deranged those elements in the human mind which led to action that there should not be a free decision as between the forces of right and forces of wrong.[52]"

At least it can be said that there are different certain kinds of reasons for practicing the right of female infanticide not only in different districts of NWP and Oudh but also in many provinces of India. As it was deliberately spread among the Indian community during the colonial era as somewhere the reasons could be identified with social, cultural, economical as well as sometimes religious also but it also differ from region to region, clan to clan and villages to villages. In fact, there is also no doubt that this practice required very prolonged and very strenuous efforts on the part of the British

Govt. in India to reduce it to its present dimensions. Thus, the institution of female infanticide consisted as one of the most important features of Indian society during colonial era. Various communities of United Province, as well of India, committed female infanticide extensively. The British Government continuously made different efforts as to suppress the evil, but in spite of this it still persisted clandestinely at a snail's pace. There was no doubt that these different kinds of evils as mentioned above kindly plays an important role in lowering the status of women in Indian social arena, as well as they reduced the opportunity of girls to avail education. Because these evils are deeply rooted in Indian society and people both male and female are less aware from educating the girls in the family, as because of it female literacy rate goes downwards instead of upward. So, it can be said that these evils affect the educational and social status of girls and women in United Provinces.

FOOTNOTES

1. Indrani Sen, Memshahib's writing, Orient black Swan, 2008, p.179
2. V. Geetha, Patriarchy, Published by Stree, kolkata, 2015, p.4
3. Ibid, p. 8
4. S. Bandyopadhyay, *From Plassey to Partition: A History of Modern India*, Orient Black swan New Delhi, 2013, p.151.
5. Parimala V. Rao, *New Perspective in the History of Indian Education*, Orient Black swan, New Delhi, 2014, p.95.
6. S. Bandyopadyay, *From Plassey to Partition: A History of Modern India*, New Delhi, 2013., p.150.
7. Charu Gupta, *Gendering Colonial India Reform, Print Caste and Communalism*, Orient Black Swan New Delhi, 2012, p.57.
8. Ibid, p. 58
9. Ibid, p. 64
10. Indrani Sen, *Memshahib's Writings*, Orient BlackSwan, New Delhi., p.126
11. Charu Gupta, *Gendering Colonial India Reform, Print Caste and Communalism*,Orient Black swan, New Delhi p.66.
12. Geraldine Forbes, *Women in Colonial India*, Chronicles Books, New Delhi, 2005., p.12

13. The Dharma Sabha was founded in Calcutta in 1830 to protest the prohibition of the rite, and took its objections to appeal before the Privy Council in London, as quoted in Charu Gupta, *Gendering Colonial India*, p.74.
14. Ibid, pp. 74-75.
15. Geraldine Forbes, *Women in Colonial India*, p.20
16. A.S. Altekar, *The Position of Women in Hindu Civilization,* Motilal Banarsidass Publishers, Delhi., p. 169.
17. Ibid.p. 169.
18. S. Bhattacharya, *ed., The Development of Women's Education in India*, Kanishka Publishers, New Delhi, 2001, p.285.
19. Ibid. pp.. 285-286.
20. File no. 85/ 1916, Emprovement of Female Education, United Provinces, Education Deptt.
21. File no. 85/ 1916, Emprovement of Female Education, United Provinces, Education Deptt .
22. Geraldine Forbes, *Women in Colonial India*, p.21.
23. Ibid. p. 21
24. Ibid. p. 22.
25. File no. 85/ 1916, Emprovement of Female Education, United Provinces, Education Deptt.
26. Ibid.
27. A.S. Altekar., *The Position of Women in Hindu Civilization From Prehistoric To Present Day*, Delhi, 2014., p.60.
28. Ibid, p. 61
29. Hansa Mehta 2nd Instalment, Printed material-3, *All India Women Conference, Anti-child marriage Committee*, Bulletin No.2, Child marriage: The existing Legislation for its prevention.
30. A.S. Altekar, *The Position of Women in Hindu Civilization From Prehistoric To Present Day*, Delhi, 2014., p.4
31. Lalita Panigrahi, *British Social Policy and Female Infanticide in India*, Munshiram Manohar lal, New Delhi, 1972., p.1
32. Ibid. pp. 4-5.
33. P.K Srivastava, *Female Infanticide in 19th Century India: A Genocide*?, Advances in historical studies, 2014,3,269-284. Accessed on 20/11/ 2015.

34. Lalita Panigrahi, *British Social Policy and Female Infanticide in India*, New Delhi, 1972., p.82.
35. Ibid. p. 89.
36. Ibid. p. 90.
37. Ibid. p. 90
38. Ibid. p. 93
39. Ibid. p. 93.
40. Thana : a police post.
41. The *Urdu Akhbar* (Akola) of 17 March 1877, Vernacular Papers, Vol. 10, p. 211.
42. The *Lawrence Gazette*, of 1871 Vernacular Papers, Vol.4,p.303.
43. Ibid. p. 303.
44. The *Aftabi Panjab* of 14th June, Vernacular papers, Vol.13.pp. 408-409
45. The Laurence Gazette, Vernacular papers, Vol.4,1871,p.305.
46. File 708, Annual report on female infanticide in the NWP for year ending 31st March 1887, Police deptt., NWP and Oudh.
47. Administrative report of NWP and Oudh, 1895-96.
48. Ibid, p. 60.
49. Administrative report of NWP and Oudh, 1899-1900.
50. From H. Tonkinson, Joint Secretary to Govt. of India to Secretary to the Government of United Provinces; Infanticide, No. f/529-25 Judicial dated January 2, 1926, file no. 213/1926, Judicial (criminal) Department, May 1926.
51. Ibid.
52. Ibid.

4

Growth of Women Education in United Provinces

In the previous chapter we discussed the various issues which hampered the women's education in the United Provinces. This chapter deals about the women education in United Provinces. It is well known fact that the British came to India just for trade and commerce, they had very little interest towards Indian education, and woman education was totally negligible at earlier stage.

N.L., Gupta Opined that," The East India Company did not consider it necessary to educate the fair-sex, perhaps because lady clerks or officers were not required for administrative purposes"[1]. Actually earlier it was the efforts of the Christian Missionaries, who really came forward for the women education. Nevertheless some efforts were made by the British government in the field of women's education by eradicating the different evils and inhuman practices in India with regard to women like Sati, female infanticide etc., through which some ray of hope was seen in terms of women's education in different provinces even in United Provinces.

The East India Company was first compelled to accept responsibility for the education of the Indian people under the Charter Act of 1813[2]. A clause was made by the East India Company's Act of 1813, enabling the governor general to devote not less than a lakh of rupees annually to education. Actually the conservative officials of the company basically restricted their educational activities to men and refused to take any direct action for the education of women. Very little amount was to be spent on the education of women. The problem basically came in front of women education was the strong prejudices against the women education, which was deeply among the native people of India in every provinces. The first attempt of the company should be restricted to the education of men who would themselves, at a later date, undertake the education of their women-folk. They also refused to grant any financial assistance to special private schools established for girls. At that time, Indian private efforts were almost exclusively meant for boys and most of the private educational institutions for girls were conducted by missionaries[3].

Macaulay's Minute

Christian missionaries had great impact and a very deep influence on education in India. Missionaries contributed a lot towards vernacular literature by their printed books in the vernacular language, along with the western subject through the medium of English. And this is what is known as "English education". The demand of English education mainly arose in the province like Bombay, Madras, Bengal by some social reformers which was deeply influenced by the western ideas. United Provinces was far lagging behind in this area. This reformation created differences between the 'Orientalists' who were in favour of traditional teaching and the 'Anglicists' who were in the favour of Western English. It was admitted on all sides that educating the masses through the medium of their own language, i.e. the vernacular, was the ultimate object to be kept in view, and in one of their annual reports, the Committee wrote, 'we conceive the formation of a vernacular literature, to be the ultimate object to which all our efforts must be directed. J. Thomson in the North-West Provinces, advocated the encouragement of vernacular teaching'.[4] 'This struggle between the Orientalists and the Anglicists led to the famous Minute of 1835 of Macaulay, then legal member of the executive council, on the side of Anglicists. It also brought about the decisive minutes of the two successive Governor-Generals, Lord William Bentick in 1835 and Lord Auckland in 1839, endorsing Maculay's policy. The schools for oriented learning were maintained, but the translations in to Sanskrit and Arabic were discontinued. The system of 'English education' was adopted and encouraged by the government, and was developed side by side with the vernacular schools[5]. By introducing English education as compulsory, the colonialist government had its own motives because by doing this they will get educated Indians which would help them in their administration. It was also assumed that this education imparted to the upper classes of the society automatically would filter down to the lower classes gradually. In other words it can be said that, the major feature of this educational policy was therefore, the theory of "downwards filtration". It was not meant for the masses, but for only "the rich, the learned, the men of business", as C.E. Trevelyan described them, as they already had a literature tradition, had eagerness as well as means to learn and above all had sufficient leisure. Once these men were trained, they could act as teachers and through them elementary education would percolate downward through regional languages at much less public expenditure. Thus, the whole indigenous society would be benefitted from Western knowledge and superior moral and ethical ideas.[6] Very less attention was paid towards the female education. There were very few schools and colleges for girls in different provinces, and NWP and Oudh were lagging far more behind in terms of girls education.

Wood's Despatch and Lord Dalhousie

In the History of education in modern India, the age of Dalhousie was very remarkable for the foundation of a modern system of education which was laid down during the administration of Dalhousie who was the Governor-General of India between, 1848-1856. Dalhousie was the first Governor-General who provided official support for female education in British India.[7]

Wood's Despatch of 1854, drafted by Northbrook, who later became the Governor-General of India, has been called as Magna Carta of Indian education. Sir Charles Wood's epoch-making despatch of 1854, basically analyzed the whole subsequent course of Indian educational development. Actually, at that point of time East India Company looked at the problem of mass education as an impossibility. The East India Company refused to give any financial support to female education. They focused only to teach and to reach up to the masses by educating them and to filter down the lower classes. The Despatch abandoned the filtration policy. The Despatch of 1854, first imposed upon the government of India the duty of creating a properly articulated system of education from the primary school to the University".[8] It also recommended the establishment of Universities at Calcutta, Madras and Bombay on the model of University of London.

The Despatch suggested that the grant-in-aid was to be given on completely religious neutrality to all schools imparting a good secular education and satisfactory local management and government inspection. On the question of trained school teachers and about text books, the Despatch paid a lot of attention towards both these things in the schools. The Despatch also recommended professional training in law, medicine and civil engineering. The Despatch also stressed upon the urgent spreading of education among women in terms of women education it is observed in paragraph 83, 'The importance of female education in India cannot be overrated and we have observed with pleasure the evidence which is now afforded of an increased desire on the part of many of the natives of India to give a good education to their daughters. The Despatch visualised that the progress of education would not only provide the government with able, efficient and faithful servants but also the possibility of such appointments would also act as an incentive to the progress of education in India'.[9]

In the North Western Province and Oudh, the despatch found only 17 girls schools with 383 pupils, all conducted by missions.[10] Naturally, these schools were small in number and the total number of girls receiving this education was very minute as compared from the total population, although a change had taken place towards female education. Later on in 1856 in some provinces like Agra, Muttra, Mynpoorie and Banda, the female education by direct instrumentality was set on foot in several districts. The cost was paid altogether by government or by a school cess. The scheme was also supported by the government and by the highest rank of officers. The apparent success was correspondingly great. It is thus described by Mr. Reid in the report for 1859-60, 'In the commencement of 1857 there were in the Agra district alone 288 female schools, containing 4927 girls. The disastrous events of 1857 absolutely distinguished them, as well as the sixteen schools with 303 girls in the Muttra district, 3 schools with 54 girls in Zillah Mynpoorie and few in the

Banda district."[11] This shows a very little progress of female education as from previous years.

Basically, female education in India inched its way through under the stewardship of individual pioneers and the missionaries because before 1854, the attitude of the authorities towards women's education was very negligible. There was not any kind of involvement towards this. Even the company was not ready to take initiative or any kind of programme towards female education. According to J.A. Richey, 'Prior to the Despatch of 1854 from the court of Directors, female education was not recognized as a branch of the state system of education in India. The attention of the authorities does not appear to have been directed to the subject until many years, after they had adopted definite measures for the education for boys. In none of the general despatches relating to educational matters submitted to or received from the Courts of Directors during the first half of the 19th century is there any reference to the education of Indian girls and women. It would seem that the authorities both in England and in India were of opinion that any attempt to introduce female education, where there was no demand for it, might be regarded by the people as an interference with their social customs.'[12]

Although Despatch did not bestow on the Indian people certain rights and privileges in education, but some of concepts of Despatch like inculcation of Indian languages, use of the mother tongue as the medium of instruction at school level, introduction of University education like law and civil, concept of mass education and of secular education in society like India.

The Despatch was criticized by M.R. Paranjpe who observed it in his Progress of education in 1941 that, 'The Despatch does not even refer to the ideal of Universal literacy although it expects education to spread over a wider field through the grant-in-aid system: it does not recognize the obligation of the state to educate every child below a certain age, it does not declare that poverty shall be no bar to the education of deserving students; and while it may be admitted that employment in government offices was not the object of English education as visualized in the Despatch, the authors did not aim at education for leadership, education for the industrial regeneration of India, education for the defense of the motherland, in short, education required by the people of a self-government nation'.[13]

Unfortunately, with lot of enthusiasm with which the Despatch of 1854 launched for its support to the education of women was not very successful and it also cannot be ignored that Despatch of 1854 provided us a platform to have some changes in education in response to the changes in our society over the years since 1854; with the disturbances of 1857 revolt, which were followed by an emphatic declaration of the policy of social and religious neutrality by Her Majesty the Queen. Lord Stanley's Despatch of 1859 also observed that 'both the difficulties and the importance of female education are adequately appreciated by the officers of the Department of Education', and invited the views of the Governor-General in council as to "the nature and degree of the influence which may safely and properly be exerted by the officers of the Department of Education to promote the extension of schools for females'.[14] Very slow progress was made towards women education, and also was not much achieved till 1870.

In the following years very little progress in terms of women education was seen in United Provinces. In North-Western Provinces, the numbers of schools are at very large in terms of schools but the main difficulty which basically comes is the way of inspection. The Agra circle contains the more number of schools with 187 with 3465 pupils. In Allahabad circle the education of girls did not make striking advance in the last year, but the progress and state of the schools may be considered satisfactory. There is a decrease of two schools and an increase of 36 pupils; and the total number of schools being 87, with an aggregate of 1554 girls, of these, 1051 are in the lowest class; 1022 are Hindus and 533 Musalmans; 888 are the children of Agriculturists, 1026 read Hindi, 44 Persian and the rest Urdu. All the teachers of these schools are women, four of them having being trained in the Benaras normal school. The majority of the girls can read and write and are acquainted with elementary arithmetic.[15] Many of the girls can read fairly and know very little about arithmetic. Same was in the case of Oudh, as in these Provinces some important changes were made in the management and in the control of girls schools. The normal schools at Lucknow never trained any women but Mahomedans. Basically, in this Province, schools and pupils have been increased, but it is difficult to ascertain the exact progress made. Thus the schools have increased by thirty-one and the pupils have risen from 879 to 1369, or have increased by 490. The average attendance per school is now about twenty; last year it was twenty-three.[16] Thus it can be said that the education of girls in Oudh is at its beset with difficulties. Very little progress was made in this way. Basically, the native gentlemen was not in the favor of girls education, they just want to keep women in Purdah system, in fact they not even cared for the instruction of education of their female children. A.P Howell mentions in his report that female schools are, in his opinion, only likely to succeed in outlying towns and villages, not in such a city as Lucknow. To a certain extent his opinion is borne out by facts. That is to say, it is both easier and cheaper to maintain a school for girls in a village or town than in Lucknow.[17]

Later on in the coming year during 1875, there were almost 100 female schools for girls which was basically attended by natives, which mainly consist of 81 government schools, 16 were aided and 3 were unaided. The table 3.1 (A) and 3.1 (B) clearly shows the comparative results of government and aided schools (detail information is given in appendix). It is said that "each pupil educated at an Aided school costs on an average more than three times as much as one educated at a government school, and costs the government more than twice as much."[18]

Table no. 3.1 (A) and 3.1 (B) gives the comparative results of Govt. and Aided Schools.

Table 3.1 (A)

Nature of School	No. of Schools	No. of Pupils per School on rolled rolls at close of the year	Average no. enrolled per school	Average Daily attendance per School	Percentage of attendance
Govt.	81	25.3	25	20.4	81.1
Aided	16	25.8	26.4	20.3	76.8

Table 3.1 (B)

Year	No. of Schools	No. of Pupils per School on rolled rolls at close of the year	Average no. enrolled	Average Daily attendance per School	Percentage of attendance
1872-1873	89	2020	2008	1604	80
1873-1874	91	2052	2031	1658	81

Source: S. Bhattacharya, ed., Development of Women's Education in India: A Collection of Documents, New Delhi, 2001.p.65.

The year opened with 89 schools, and basically closed by 81. This year can be called as the year of progress; for, though the number of schools has decreased by 8, the average daily attendance has increased by 46. Mr. Thomson, respecting the female schools in his circle remarks that "these schools have had all the success that was expected of them". It is remarked that, female schools can be a good deal and more expensive than boys. Now the question arises why female education was more expensive than boys? The reason is that firstly, the schools were situated very far from their native places. Secondly, because of this parents were insecure to send their daughters at a very far place. Thirdly, the old orthodox thinking of the male counter-parts of not having educated wives and daughters.

As compared to other provinces, women were not very free in Oudh, the education of women remains a strictly private as well as a domestic question where guardians did not pay any attention towards the education of women. Different sources told that during the last year's report there was the decrease of 52 in girls and an increase of 49 in halkabandi schools (govt. primary vernacular schools). Condition of girls education was sometime up and down. Later on in year 1876 the no. of girls schools has decreased from 375 to 316, and there appears to be some improvements in teaching in those that remain'.[19]

Further in the year 1877-78, the government schools are all of the lower or primary class. About the aided schools in the N-W Provinces 5 are middle schools for European girls with 359 pupils, 4 are middle schools for native girls with 445 on the rolls and 128 are primary schools with 2933 pupils. The number attending the government schools has fallen from 2662 in 1876-77 to 2633 in the year under report.[20] Thus, we can see there is a decrease in attending the schools of government. From the 3.2 table given below show the general statement about the no. of schools and on roll girls during 1877-78, on 31st March.

Table 3.2

No. of schools and on roll of girls during 1877-78, on 31st March

Schools	No. Of Schools	Roll, 1877-78, 31st March			
		Hindus	Muslims	Others	Total
N.W. Provinces					
Government	107	2115	477	41	2633
Aided	143	1483	1342	1451	4276
Private	-	-	-	-	-
Total	250	3598	1819	1492	6909
Oudh					
Government	65	737	870	2	1609
Aided	18	160	493	93	746
Private	4	40	54	-	94
Total	87	937	1417	95	2449
Grand Total	**337**	**4535**	**3236**	**1587**	**9358**

Source: S. Bhattacharya, The Development of Women's Education in India.

The condition related to women education mainly differs from one province to other provinces. The female schools in Oudh division was almost dozen in number and due to report of inspector of the Oudh division says that the girls schools of Oudh not properly attended, and are in better order and better taught that the generality of girls schools with which I made acquaintance in North-Western Provinces. Even the girls schools in the Hardoi districts seem upon the whole to be the best, and those in Sitapur to be next best.[21] This statement seems that in these two districts the status of women education was very satisfactory. Next, the report says that, the schools in the Lucknow city under the charge of Mrs. Massin, the deputy inspectress, have made little progress this year. Many of the girls in these schools are parda-nashin, who have to be carried to and from work by doolie-bearers attached to the schools as part of the establishment. We do not expect therefore more than a small attendance at these schools, but even the small attendance expected has hardly been reached this year.[22] From the report of Mrs. Masih its clear that girls education was making progress but no doubt very slow in this term. Somewhere the attendance was falling off. During the year 1871 and 1881, a great decrease took place in girls schools.

It assumed that the decrease was mainly due to the financial position of the government in 1876, because mainly in this year there were 400 government primary schools for girls, with 9000 pupils in the North-Western Provinces and Oudh.[23] So it can be felt that very much progress was made in the field of women education up to1881.[24]

Hunter Commission (1882)

A careful perusal of the developments in education in British India since 1855 reveals that many of these were not in accordance with the provisions of the educational Despatch of 1854. Contrary of the expectation of the Despatch, the government did not only withdraw from the field of education but also failed to build up a system of mass education through grant-in-aid. As a matter of fact, elementary education was much neglected at the expense of secondary and higher education. All these were certainly grounds for a review of the educational developments in the country since 1855 but the matter was actually hastened by the Christian missionaries.

The educational growth which was continuously prevailing at the previous period was not up to the expectations among the masses, as it did not focus on primary education and private enterprises was also being crushed. For this basically, in 1882 an education commission was appointed to inquire the whole system on the manner on which the Wood's Despatch has been adopted. In February 1882 Lord Ripon appointed the first Indian Education Commission with William Hunter, a member of his executive council, as its chairman. The commission was asked "to enquire particularly in to the Despatch of 1854, and to suggest such measures as it might think desirable with a view to the further carrying out of the policy there in laid down. The commission was asked to be more focused on primary education as it was mere lagging behind among women. The Indian education commission very briefly discussed the problems of the education of women with great insight, as women education was extremely in backward condition. As earlier there was no demand for women education . Basically, the system of child marriage, drop out many girls with large portion from schools at an very early age, so it discarded them as to complete their education. This, on the whole decreases in the supply of female teachers in girls schools. Due to which parents basically withdraws their daughters mainly from schools, which was one of the major drawback in terms of women education. As this also employs male teachers in to the girls schools. As regards the improper instruction, and the unsuitable framing of textbook also one of the major drawback in terms of girls education, as it does not met at the requirement of education of girls. All these several reasons proved that there is less education in all different provinces of India and mainly in United Provinces, as there was less awareness among the people about women education.

In order to remove several difficulties, which stood as obstacles in the way towards women's education, the Indian Education Commission recommended different suggestions for improving the state of girls education in general. It can be said that these suggestions did not mark out any new line of policy, but supposed to be tentative and provisional. In fact, Indian education commission very minutely observed the different problems which our Indian women faced in perceiving education: (1) the commission after accepting that female education should be treated as a legitimate charge on provincial, local and municipal funds and should receive special arrangements. (2) the principle of aiding indigenous schools be recognised as an important means of extending elementary education. (3) the grant-in-aid code system in different provinces should be revised as to afford aid to girls schools on easier terms as regards rate of aid, the attendance of scholars, the standards of instruction, fees scholarships, provision of boarding accommodation. (4) primary education should be extended in backward districts (5) in all different provinces the system of scholarships should be encouraged (6) grants-in-aid were given with un discriminating liberality to all promoters of girls school (7) the establishment of stipendiary pupil teacher-ships (8) formal recognition of grants for zenana teaching as a proper charge on public funds. (9) basically for girls there should be special system of scholarship for girls. (10) provision for pupil-teachers and encouragement of additional normal schools. (11) there should be larger employment of female inspecting agency. (12) additional training schools for women should be provided, and liberal aid afforded to those under private management. (13) girls schools were not to be placed under the management of local boards or municipalities, except at the desire of those bodies, and even then, the control was to be surrounded by certain safeguards. (14) mixed schools other than infant schools, not being suited to the condition of the country, should not therefore, be encouraged except in places where girls schools could not be maintained. (15) It also suggests the establishment of an alternative standard for high schools, corresponding to the matriculation examinations, but should have no relation to any other course of any University.[25]

The government of the NWP and Oudh felt that the recommendation of the Commission, for the furtherance of female education, may be accepted in their entirety as laying down temporarily and judiciously the lines on which further action in this difficult and important matter should proceed.[26] The Lt. Governor of NWP and Oudh, Sir Alfred C. Lyall,[27] concurred with the Commission that keeping in the existing circumstances of the women of India, the mere establishment of schools will be by no means sufficient to bring about the general spread of education among them; that is to say, that in their case public instruction, which can exist only by the establishment of public institutions, is in itself of but little use. Female education is, of all branches of the subject, that to which public instruction is least applicable, it is that in which the difficulties are greatest and the results hardest to verify. Before any considerable progress can be attained, the natives must themselves, and a public opinion less indifferent to the education of women, must be formed'.[28]

In accordance with the recommendations of the Commission the Provinces were supposed to increase the educational percentage, either from private enterprise or from the provincial board, in order with an increased provision of funds for primary education especially girls education. However, it appear that 84 percent of the local, 74 percent of the municipal, and 21 percent of the provincial funds, devoted to education, was expanded on primary education in the NWP and Oudh in the year 1881-82.[29]

Up to 1871 and 1881, a great decline took place in girls schools. The main reason was due to the financial position of the government in 1876. However, it was felt that if changes were necessary, then it could be possible with the least prejudices to education. The total no. of girls schools in 1882 was 308, attended by 8883 pupils. The returns, in the last annual reports of the Department, shows a small increase both in schools and scholars, and in instruction also there are signs of improvements.'[30]

Special difficulties attended the cause of female education in the Oudh districts. Here table 3.3 gives the detail of female education as mention above and exact number of institutions and number of pupils in different government institutions and in other institutions.

Table 3.3

Female Education in the North-Western Provinces and Oudh in 1882

	Government Institution			**Other Institutions, Aided, and Unaided (Under inspection)**			**Mixed Schools**	**Total**	**Total Expenditure**
	Normal Schools	Secondary Schools	Primary Schools	Normal Schools	Secondary Schools	Primary Schools			
No. Of Institutions	-	-	160	3	3	142	-	308	Rs. 79082
No. Of Pupils	-	-	3687	89	68	5039	-	8883	-

Source: S. Bhattacharya, the Development of Women's Education in India, p.118.

In 1881, according to the Census Returns there is aggregate increase in female education for all India during the past ten years. This increase has been fairly spread over the larger provinces, except in Punjab and NWP and Oudh. Next major attention has been made to the primary education of girls as compared to secondary or higher education. Throughout India, the total number of pupils in government girls primary schools is 23850 or one half of those in aided or unaided schools under inspection, namely, 58570. And in NWP and Oudh the proportion is 3.5 to 5. NWP and Oudh basically lags behind so much as compared to other provinces. There were very less girls under instruction as compared to other provinces. To understand it briefly see table 3.4.

Table 3.4

Female Education in British India in 1881, according to the Census Returns.

Province	Total female Population	No. of girls under instruction	No. of females not under instruction but able to read and write	Proportion to Total female population	
				Girls under instruction	Females who can read and write but not under instruction
Madras	15,749,588	39,104	94,571	1 in 403	1 in 166
Bombay	7,956,696	18,460	32,648	1 in 431	1 in 244
Bengal	34,911,270	35,760	61,449	1 in 976	1 in 578
NWP and Oudh	21,195,313	9,771	21,590	1 in 2,169	1 in 981
Punjab	8,640,384	6,101	8,407	1 in 1,416	1 in 1,028
CP	4,879,356	3,171	4,187	1 in 1,539	1 in 1,165
Assam	2,377,723	1,068	1,786	1 in 2,226	1 in 1,331
Coorg	77,863	431	356	1 in 180	1 in 219
Haidarabad Assigned Districts	1,292,181	356	789	1 in 3,630	1 in 1,638
Total	97,080,374	114,222	225,783	1 in 849	1 in 430

Source: S. Bhattacharya, ed., Development of Women's Education in India: A Collection of Documents, New Delhi, 2001, p.125.

Above table 3.4 clearly shows female education in British India in 1881, as according to the Census Returns. In the progress of female education there were many problems. There were many obstacles in their way as summarized by Indian Commission like: (1) There is no demand of education in case of girls and women. (2) The ever going continuance of different evils like female infanticide, child marriage, purdah system etc. nearly hampers the education and future of Indian girls. (3) The inadequate supply of female teachers in girls schools due to which parents had objection in sending their girls child to schools. (4) The schools were situated at very far places from their houses. (5) The state system of instruction, control agencies, inspection and text-books are the several factors which does not meet up to the requirements of girls education. (6) The less support from native gentlemen in favour of women education hampers the women education, as they don't want to see them as a educated lady as equal to them.

In the NWP, Sir Alfred Lyall was of the opinion that mere establishment of schools would do little towards the spread of education among women; "before any considerable progress is obtained, the natives must themselves lend their cooperation and full assent to the administrative measures of Govt., and a public opinion less indifferent to the education of women must be formed."[31]

Primary Education for Girls

There were lots of difficulties in the way of female education due to which large number of girls withdraws themselves from very primary stage. Basically, the system of child marriage was one of the major drawback in terms of girls education, as it draws large proportion of the girls from school at a very early age and this cuts off them from receiving education.

Table 3.5

Figures of Girls in P.S. in NWP and Oudh for the years 1886-87 and 1891-92.

1886-1887														
Province	Maintained by the Department		Maintained by local and Municipal Boards		Maintain by Native States		Aided		Unaided		Total		Girls in Boys Schools	Boys in Girls Schools
	Schools	Pupils	Schools	Pupils	Schools	Pupils	Schools	Pupils	Schools	Pupils	Schools	Pupils		
N-WP and Oudh	-	-	168	3753	-	-	159	5527	17	381	344	9661	-	-
1891-1892														
N-WP and Oudh	-	-	136	2917	-	-	167	5832	11	353	314	9102	217	317

Source: A.M. Nashq, Progress of Education in India 1887-88 to 1891-92, Second Quinquennial Review.

This table clearly shows the number of schools and girls schools in different instruction in different years and NWP and Oudh shows a decrease both in schools and scholars. There was an increment in the boys schools as compared to girls schools. It is to note worthy that in some provinces along with the NWP and Oudh province the girls education shows no increase in primary education. "In the N-W schools shows a decrease, while pupils are stationary; but this poor return is distinctly better than that for the previous five years when both schools and pupils decreased considerably."[32]

In the year 1891-92 total no. of public institutions for girls was 5711 and in private institutions was 1042. Next in the year 1896-97 the total no. of public institutions was 6550 and of private institution was 1458. Next in the year 1901-02 the public institutions was 6176 and private institutions were 1338. This is the data of total no. of public and private institutions for girls during the year from 1891-1902. Now, among this, the total number of public institutions and private institutions for girls during the year from 1891-1902 was 395 and 176 respectively."[33] The NWP shows a decrease in both schools and scholars. In fact, in both aided and unaided primary schools there was seen an era of decline towards the primary education. J.S. Cotton report discussed it as observed by the Deputy inspectors in several districts as well in NWP and Oudh and widely reports state that "the girls in the primary schools are quite young children and therefore, purdah is not always insisted on; the inspection then takes place in the same way as for boys, except that it is held in the school and not at an open air centre. When purdah is insisted on, the girls are made to sit behind a curtain and the answers may be given with assistance which cannot be detected. Hence, no satisfactory inspection can be conducted by a male officer, and it would be well if females could be employed; but the schools in a district are usually too few for the employment of an inspectress. Sometimes the managers of Mission schools object to the inspection being conducted by the deputy inspector, possibly from want of confidence in the impartiality of that officer in judging schools under Christian management".[34] These lines interpret that Purdah system basically hampers the girls education at an very early age. As the results shows that the NWP and Oudh did not have satisfactory progress as compared to other provinces. Due to several obstacles in the way towards women education, the women of NWP and Oudh are lagging behind as compared to other province, but year by year slowly they are making little progress, a step of increment can be seen in their progress. In fact girls education has now gained the first place for consideration in all schemes for expansion, as table 3.6 from the year 1931-1937 shows a continuous increment in the no. of girls in United Provinces.

Table 3.6

Total number of girls pupils in all institutions

Provinces	No. of girls pupils in		
	1931-32	1936-37	Increase in the no. of girls
United Provinces	167011	224688	57677

Source: John Sargent, Progress of Education in India, 1932-1937.

Above table clearly gives the pictures about the enrollment of girls in the given time period, and there is an account of increment in the no. of girls. However, this shows that there is want of desire of women education in the provinces. 'In the United provinces the large increase in enrollment at the primary stage is due to the encouragement given by inspecting officers and others, and to the removal from the Educational code of the rule, which had hitherto restricted girls beyond a certain age from reading in boys schools'[35] Here table 3.7 which is listed below is showing briefly the no. of institutions and no. of scholars in it regarding to Primary education.

Table 3.7

No. of Institutions and students during the year 1902-33 in Primary education in United Provinces

Year	No. of Institutions	Increase (+) Decrease(-)	No. of Scholars	Increase(+) Decrease (-)
1902	429	Not available	14807	+
1906	Not available	Not available	Not available	+
1908	930	+	Not available	Not available
1909	936	+	Not available	Not available
1911	Not available	Not available	+	Not available
1912	55	Not available	+	Not available
1913	1062	+	2162	+
1914	Increased by 18	+	By 416	+

(Contd...)

1915	17239	+	993549	+
1916	18122	+	1036125	+
1917	142203	+	5818730	+
1918	12653	+	725462	+
1919	1222	+	41624	+
1920	By 40	+	42869	+
1923	Not available	+	Not available	+
1924	Not satisfactory	-	Not available	-
1925	1563	+	52534	+
1926	1568	+	54118	+
1927	1657	+	57478	+
1928	Not available	-	59451	+
1929	1711	-	Not available	-
1931	1719	-	Not available	-
1932	1773	-	Not available	-

Source: Estimated from Administration reports of United Province and Statistics reports.

The table given above clearly gives the clear picture of number of institutions and no. of students in the institution at primary stage. Certain years show basically the unsatisfactory results regarding institutions and scholars. Basically year 1924 gives the unsatisfactory result regarding the number of institutions and there can also be seen a decrease in the number of scholars also. As earlier in 1909, the number of institutions established was around 936 but no particular data was available regarding the number of scholars but from the sources it was assumed that there was the decline in the number of scholars at primary level. Again in the year 1923 no particular data was available to show the number of institutions and number of students but from the reports of administration says that there was the increment in both i.e. in the number of institutions as well as in the number of scholars. If we talk about the overall view of the status of girls education at primary level from 1902 up to 1932 it was found that there was the expansion of primary education among girls, as the expansion was not at very high level but yes progress was there at this stage. The percentage of increment was more or less was not very excellent. Still, there was a need to extent the schools in the provinces.

Compulsory Primary Education

To make primary education more progressive different measures were taken by the government of united Provinces. For example in 1923, compulsory primary education act was made in Sitapur municipality. According to the census taken in Feb.1927 there were 1429 boys of the age between 6 and 11 years, but in the last census taken in Feb. 1928 the number has decreased to 1356. In the year under the report the Board secured an enrollment of 97% of the boys residing in the compulsion area.'[36] The above lines describes about the percentage of boys, as there was no mention about the girls education. Again in 1921, in the Cawnpore Municipality there are 'approximately 10,000 boys between the ages of 6 and 11 years and of these 3,000 or 30% are now attending vernacular primary schools'[37]. These data interpret that there were more focus on boys education in these districts (Sitapur and Cawnpore), as no data were available on girls education in these districts in the particular year.

To fill these gaps in the Primary Education, UNITED PROVINCES DISTRICT BOARDS PRIMARY EDUCATION ACT, 1926 was introduced as to make growth in primary education in the provinces. This particular Act aims at:

> 'To provide for the extension of primary education in rural areas under district boards in the United Province District Boards Primary Education Act, 1926. It declared the policy of the government of the United Provinces that universal, free and complusory primary education for boys and girls should be reached by a definite programme of progressive expansion and whereas it is expedient to provide for a progressive development and expansion of primary education. It extends to all the areas under the jurisdiction of the district boards in the United Province. According to this act primary education means instruction in reading, writing, and arithmetic of such standard as may be prescribed for primary schools by the local government. Basically, the United Province are backward in primary education, the percentage of boys of school-going age

receiving primary education in rural areas being only 25, while that of girls is much smaller. It means the condition of girls education regarding primary was unsatisfactory. The need for progress is thus obvious and is all the more necessary because, since the introduction of the constitution reforms the education of the masses has recognized as one of the essentials for political growth. The Govt. are therefore, anxious to spread education among the masses, as in order to ensure a wide and rapid diffusion of knowledge among them some complusion meausres are to be taken. In almost all civilized countries elementary education is compulsory."[38]

With the Act of United Province District Boards Primary Education Act of 1926 made a several changes in many district of United Provinces. Many of the District during coming years made girls education compulsory in many district, while on the other hand many had several problems in enforcing this Act. As in 1935, DPI (Director of Public Instruction) of United Provinces directed to Governor as ' to approve the introduction of compulsory Primary Education for Girls from September 11, 1935 in the four wards of the Cawnpore Municipality:

1. Moulganj
2. Patkapur
3. Sadar Bazar
4. Anwarganj

As in these wards of Cawnpore Municipality Compulsory Primary Education was enforced along with the direction that a lady superintendent should be appointed for this'.[39] This step taken by DPI shows that the Govt. are also now enthusiastic to improve the condition of girls education at primary level. As according to the Census taken in May 1933, it reveals that 'there were 5,306 girls between the ages of 6 and 11 years in these wards'[40]. As table 3.8 clearly gives the no. of girls in these 4 wards of Cawnpore municipality.

Table 3.8

No. of girls in the four wards of Cawnpore Municipality in the year 1933

	Girls		**Total**	**Boys**
	Hindus	**Muslim**		
Patkapur	1025	180	1205	2128
Sadar Bazar	1005	115	1120	2107
Moulganj	638	383	1021	1612
Anwarganj	965	995	1960	3746
Total	3633	1673	5306	9593

Source: File no.1136 of 1935, Compulsory Primary Education for Girls in Cawnpore Municipality, Education Deptt.

From above table then we will found that total no. of girl is 5306 and of boys are 9593, undoubtedly there is a variation between the no. of girls in compulsory Primary Education as compared to boys. But yes a step was taken by enforcing the compulsory Primary Education Act and definitely a progress will be seen in this field. Later on in the year 1934-35 there are some both rural and urban areas where compulsory girls primary education was enforced, they are in Municipal Boards the districts which covered were:

1. Sikandarabad
2. Allahabad
3. Muttra
4. Cawnpore and

In District Boards the districts which covered were:

1. Etawah
2. Gorakhpur
3. Lucknow
4. Garhwal

These are the some district where compulsory Primary Education of girls introduced during the year 1934'.[41] The expansion of this compulsory Act reveals that in coming years there was the demand of girls primary education. Apart from these districts like Sikandarabad, Allahabad, Muttra, Mirzapur, Cawnpore, Etawah, Gorakhpur, Lucknow, Garhwal, there are some districts where also this act did not felt important to introduce it. 'Balrampur in the opinion of the Board as this is not the fit time and suitable for the introduction of compulsory education for the girls. Likewise education Committee of Gorakhpur is also not in favour to introduce compulsory girls education. Bijnor was not in favour of introducing it.'[42] These certain districts are of opinion as not to introduce girls compulsory Primary Education. However, it can be assumed that these districts were least interested in girls education. After the Unite Provinces District Boards Primary Education Act, 1926 'the Govt. are pleased to notify that primary education of girls, whose ages are not less than 6 years and not more than 11 yrs (in the case of Muslim girls, not less than 5 and not more than 9 yrs) shall be compulsory in the Itaunja and Kakori village areas of the Lucknow district, with effect from 29th April 1936. As there are 386 no. of girls between 6 and 11 yrs. of age (in the case of Muslim girls 5 to 9 yrs of age) according to the census that taken in Sept, 1934. There are 77 no. of girls of these ages who are likely to be exempted. 37 no. of other girls who will continue to read in girls schools in the compulsory area.[43]

These data represents that there is desire of girls education even in rural areas like Itaunja and Kakori like villages. No doubt, these no. are very less as compared to boys, but still progress was in the way towards girls education. As boys compulsory education was introduced in every districts. As compared to this along with so many difficulties in some districts in fact in some rural and urban areas the girls compulsory education Act was enforced. Girls education was also more important as compared to boys.

Here are the some opinion through different newspaper regarding the proposal to introduce compulsory primary education for girls in rural and urban areas. A Urdu newspaper called as "Sarfaraaz" dt. 17/8/33 says that 'the municipality has shown little progress in its existing secondary and lower primary schools to justify its insistance on compulsory education for girls'.[44] 'Another in "Al-Waiz" dated 24-8-33, protesting against the proposal in Lucknow municipality boards to introduce compulsion for girls in the Wazirganj wards and says that the Muslims are in favour of giving only such education as their religion ordains and is essential for making their females good house-wives. As it want only religious education for girls. Another one called "Haqiqat" dated 10-8-33 of Lucknow utters that parents (muslims) had the objection to send their daughters if there were no religious education imparted to them. It advises, that it is better that girls education should not be made compulsory until the experiment with boys has succeeded.'[45] All these three newspapers published from Lucknow municipality where girls compulsory education was introduced in rural areas like Itaunja and Kakori villages. But most of the Muslim families had the objection to send their daughters in these schools where there is less focus on religious teaching. As they demand that there must be religious teaching. Same in Cawnpore municipality, the "Iqdam" newspaper dated 22/8/33 of Cawnpore stating that schools for Muslim girls should be separated from those of non-muslims. They also demand that there should be at least one religious Muslim teacher should be appointed in every municipal school to impart religious education and training. Another in "Gharih" dated 21/8/33 by Mr. Fakhruddin urging that if compulsion is introduced for girls, it should be seen that schools provide all kinds of facilities for imparting religious education to muslims. Next in "Sadaqat" dated 23/8/33 of Cawnpore denounces the agitation against compulsory education for girls as non ensical and based on narrow-mindedness and selfish motives. Further translation of note published by Ajit in the "Pratap" dated 3/9/33 of Cawnpore says that as Indian women are backward in education, introduction of compulsory primary education is more necessary for girls than for boys. Another one "Al-Barid" of Cawnpore dated 25/8/33, pointing out that if religious education is made compulsory the courses of study are fixed in consultation with "Ulemas" the Purdah is observed and Muslim mistress are appointed to teach the girls etc., there would certainly be no opposition from muslims quarters.'[46] These are certain views of different newspapers regarding girls compulsory education which has some objection and with some demands. As it can be said that with the introduction of girls compulsory education acted as a milestone in enhancing the primary education among girls in different districts of United Provinces.

Secondary Education among Girls

Secondary education may be defined as 'the stepping stone of the educational system' in any country. In actual to define secondary education is quite impossible. In the report of the education commission, secondary education was described as 'that which leads up from the primary to the collegiate course'.[47] Basically it is from the high schools that Universities and colleges pick the pick the country's future leaders of thought, science, statesmanship and business enterprise. That is why it is reasonable to get in to the detail of secondary education in India as well as in United Provinces. The expansion of secondary education in India dates very back in 1854 when the Wood's Despatch was published. It mainly emphasized that 'efforts should be made to extend far more widely the means of acquiring general European knowledge of a less higher order, but of such a character as may be practically useful to the people of India in their different spheres of life. So the Despatch mainly put emphasis on the establishment of schools in every district 'whose object should be not to train highly a few youths, but to provide more opportunities than now exist for the acquisition of such an improved education as will make those who possess it more useful members of society in every condition of life'.[48] It was later on, there was an increase in secondary schools and besides the efforts of provincial governments, both local bodies and private agencies started several high schools in every part of the country.

Secondary education in India was classified in to 2 stages-(1) Middle and (2) High. The Middle stage basically served the purpose of a complete course in itself while the High stage led the students to enter in the colleges and universities. Middle schools were of two types-(1) Vernacular Middle schools, and (2) English Middle schools. The distinction between these two types of schools was that the 'English' was a compulsory subject in English middle schools while in Vernacular Middle schools it was optional.[49]

Table 3.9

Number of Institution and pupils in Secondary Schools in North-Western Provinces and Oudh in 1882

	Government Institutions	Other Institutions, Aided and Unaided (Under inspection)
	Secondary Schools	Secondary Schools
No. Of Institutions	-	3
No. Of Pupils	-	68

Source: S. Bhattacharya, The Development of Women's Education in India, p.118

The above table clearly shows the number of institution and pupils and the result was that there was no institution and pupils in government institution, in fact there was some number of institution and pupils in aided and unaided institution. The status of female education in NWP and Oudh was not very satisfactory, as many factors were responsible for it. According to the Census Returns of 1881, there was a great aggregate increase in female education for all India during the past ten years. This increase of mainly in female education can be seen in every provinces, with the exception of the Punjab and NWP and Oudh. Here is the table given below showing the female Education in British India in 1882 especially in NWP and Oudh.

Table 3.10

Female Education in British India in 1882 (especially in NWP and Oudh) in terms of number of Institution and Scholars on March 31st 1882

Province	Class of Institutions	Number of Institution					Number of Scholars in					
		Departmental	Aided	Unaided under Inspection	Unaided not under Inspection	Total	Departmental	Aided Schools	Unaided under Inspection	Unaided not under Inspection	Total	Percentage of Schools to total female population of school going age
North Western Provinces and Oudh	Secondary Schools	-	3	-	-	3	-	68	-	-	68	-
	Primary	160	132	10	-	302	3687	4797	242	-	8726	27
	Mixed	-	-	-	-	-	-	-	-	-	-	-
	Normal	-	3	-	-	3	-	138	-	-	138	0.1
	Total	145	166	-	-	311	3857	5496	-	-	9353	0.72

Source: The Development of Women's Education in India: A Collection of Documents 1850-1920, P. 127.

Above table 3.10 basically shows the number of Institution for secondary education and scholars in it in the year 1882. As it clear there were very less number of girls institution in the provinces as there were only 3 aided institution for girls education in NWP and Oudh Province and as same the condition about the number of scholars in it. There are only 68 scholars in aided schools. Undoubtedly, the condition was very unsatisfactory but yes progress was still going on in this field. Later on with the passage of time some changes were made in the secondary education.

Table 3.11

Secondary Schools for Girls in 1885-86 in NWP and Oudh

Province	Managed by the Department		Managed by the local and Municipal board		Aided		Unaided		Total		Remarks
	Schools	Pupils	Schools	Pupils	Schools	Pupils	Schools	Pupils	Schools	Pupils	Girls in Boys Schools
N.W. Provinces											
English	-	-	-	-	17	1443	3	68	20	1511	-
Vernacular	-	-	-	-	2	157	-	-	2	157	-

Source: S. Bhattacharya, The Development of Women's Education in India, p.161.

The above table clearly shows the number of girls in secondary schools. As from the last five years if it is compared then for sure a line of increment was able to seen in the table. As it shows the increased no. of schools which was very less as compared last five years back. Certain changes were made in unaided institution in terms of girls secondary schools. Girls education basically hampers by the social prejudices which was only meant for them. Women education was very much weaker in a country like India, and that too especially in NWP and Oudh Province as compared to other Province. Reasons were many like the system of child-marriage withdraws many girls at an very early age, next was the supply of insufficient teachers etc.

so the reasons as counted were many which create obstacles in the way of female education. Again and again through different educational surveys it was found that in terms of girls education the NWP and Oudh province was very slow.

Later on in the year from 1887 several progress was made. Basically all the other secondary schools in the NWP and Oudh Province, except those for European schools are managed by the various missions. Later on the Director says, 'the vernacular schools are on a very different footing. Almost all the girls attending these schools are Native Christians, with whom are sometime associated East India girls of the poorest class and occasionally Parsi girls. These schools are becoming more and more important; and from what I myself seen of those at Gonda, Sitapur, Fyazabad and Lucknow they appear to contain the germs of much future promise'[50]. These above lines interpret that there was the demand of secondary schools among these districts.

Table 3.12

Secondary Schools for Girls during the year 1886-87 and 1891-92 especially in NWP and Oudh province

1886-1887												
Province	Managed by the Department		Managed by the local and Municipal board		Maintained by the native states		Aided		Unaided		Total	
	Schools	Pupils	Schools	Pupils	Schools	Pupils	Schools	Pupils	Schools	Pupils	Schools	Pupils
N.W. Provinces												
English	-	-	-	-	-	-	17	1176	-	-	17	1176
Vernacular	-	-	-	-	-	-	2	396	-	-	2	396

(Contd...)

1891- 1892												
Province	**Managed by the Government**		**Managed by the local and Municipal board**		**Maintained by the native states**		**Aided**		**Unaided**		**Total**	
	Schools	**Pupils**	**Schools**	**Pupils**	**Schools**	**Pupils**	**Schools**	**Pupils**	**Schools**	**Pupils**	**Schools**	**Pupils**
N.W. Provinces												
English	-	-	-	-	-	-	31	1836	-	-	21	1836
Vernacular	-	-	1	22	-	-	-	-	-	-		22

Source: S. Bhattacharya, The Development of Women's Education in India, p.221.

By the data of the year 1886-87 to 1891-92 on total we can see the increment in the number of pupils in English Schools while there was a decrease in the Veranacular schools came down up to 22 in the year 1891-92. Basically, ' the average strength of secondary English schools on the whole has increased schools has decreased slightly- from 78 to 77'[51]. Later on with the passage on time an increase can be seen in the progress of girls education, as table given below indicates.

Table 3.13

Girls in Secondary Schools for Indians according to stages of instruction, in the year, 1896-97

Province	High	Middle
Madras	138	2399
Bombay	215	492
Bengal	141	329
NWP and Oudh	26	211
Punjab	21	169
Central Provinces	-	55
Burma	6	303
Assam	3	9
Coorg	-	-
Berar	-	31
Total	550	3998
Total for 1891-1892	415	3452
Percentage of Increase	32	16

Source: J.S. Cotton, Progress of Education in India, 1891-93 to 1896-97.

The above table clearly shows the girls in S.S (secondary schools) in NWP and Oudh in the year of 1896-97. As in high stages there were 26 girls in NWP and Oudh and 211 in middle stages. No doubt there was an increment in the number but yes the result of NWP and Oudh was not very much satisfactory as compared to others provinces. Over all an increment by 32 in High stages and also increment by 16 in middle stages can be seen and over all there was the proportionate rate of increase in the high stage is satisfactory among Indian girls. Going back go ten years, the total no. of English Secondary Schools for girls shows little changes as over all in India. On the whole in the earlier period it fell from 244 to 232, and then rose slightly to 236. The total number of pupils in them, has however, steadily risen from 16,072 to 19,636, the rate of increase in the later period being 5 percent[52].

Table 3.14

Secondary Schools for Girls, English and Vernacular, 1891-92 and in 1896-97

1891- 1892												
Province	Government		District and Municipal		Native states		Aided		Unaided		Total	
	School	Pupil	School	Pupil	School	Pupil	Schools	Pupils	School	Pupil	School	Pupil
N.W. P. and Oudh												
English	-	-	-	-	-	-	31	1,836	-	-	21	1,836
Vernacular	-	-	-	-	-	-	-	-	-	-	1	22

1896-1897														
Province	Government		District and Municipal		Native states		Aided		Unaided		Total		Percentage of Increase or Decrease, 1896-97 compared with 1891-92	
	School	Pupil	School	Pupil	School	Pupil	Schools	Pupils	School	Pupil	School	Pupil	School	Pupil
N.W. P. and Oudh														
English	-	-	-	-	-	-	31	1,836	-	-	21	1,836	+52	+60
Vernacular	-	-	-	-	-	-	-	-	-	-	1	22	+100	+159

Source: J.S.Cotton., Progress of Education in India 1892-93 to 1896-97

As from 1891 up to 1897 there was a sign of increment in the secondary schools for girls. During this time period of span in the English schools an increase by 52 can be seen and by +60 an increment can be seen in the number of pupils in it. Same in the case of vernacular there was an increment by 100 and by pupil there was an increment of 159. These figures shows a respective increase in the number of secondary schools in the NWP and Oudh and definitely in pupils also.

Later on from 1897 up to 1902 an overall increment can be seen in the secondary schools for girls managed by different class of management. Overall in India the progress can be seen as mentioned by R. Nathan in his report.

Table 3.15

Secondary schools for girls by category of management

Province	Government	Native State	Aided	Unaided	Total	Total Public Management	Total private Management
Madras	48	1	-	5	197	49	148
Bombay	2	1	1	5	67	4	63
Bengal	3	-	-	6	59	3	56
United Provinces	-	2	-	4	40	2	38
Punjab	2	5	-	1	34	7	27
NWFP	-	-	-	-	-	-	-
Burma	-	-	-	-	39	-	39
Central Provinces	-	1	-	-	20	1	19
Assam	-	-	-	2	5	-	5
Berar	-	-	-	-	-	-	-
Coorg	-	-	-	-	-	-	-
Total,1901-02	55	10	1	23	461	66	395
Total, 1896-97	50	12	1	16	16	63	377

Source: R. Nathan., Progress of Education in India 1897-98 to 1901-02.

Therefore, according to the R. Nathan report of Progress of education in India, shows the progress of secondary schools for girls as shown in the above table. As above table shows the statistics figure of secondary schools in the United provinces and in other provinces also. No doubt the U.P still lagging far behind as compared with Madras, Bombay, Bengal etc. The condition in the several other provinces like NWFP, Burma, CP, Assam, Berar and Coorg was no better. Over in India country progress can be seen in the year 1901-1902 as compared from 1896-97.

Table 3.16

Number of girls in the high, middle stages of secondary schools

Province	**High**	**Middle**	**Total**
Madras	491	3575	4066
Bombay	610	1389	1999
Bengal	230	884	1114
United Provinces	154	716	870
Punjab	80	547	627
NWFP	-	-	-
Burma	85	650	735
Central Provinces	24	305	329
Assam	2	20	22
Berar	1	43	44
Coorg	-	4	4
Total for 1901-1902	1677	8133	9810
Total, 1896-1897	1190	7178	8368

Source: R. Nathan., Progress of Education in India, 1897-98 to 1901-02.

The table mentioned above gives the statistical figure of girls in high and middle stages of secondary schools. As according to this table there were 154 girls in high and 716 girls in middle stages in U.P. Progress can be seen in these provinces but not very satisfactory. Later on in the year of '1909-10, 1910-11, 1911-12, 1912-13, 1913-14 the number of institutions for females was 58, 61, 72, 73 and 85 for respective years. The number of female scholars in 1909-10 was 58, in 1910-11 was 61, 1911-12 was 72, 1912-13 was 73 and for 1913-14 yr the number was 85 in United provinces of Agra and Oudh.'[53] In the year '1915-16, the secondary female schools rose from 606 to 645 and scholars from 87,194 to 93,997, all the provinces contributing to the increase, as the number was fairly large in the United provinces (95)'.[54] These data interprets that there was an increment in the secondary education among girls. From the next five years there was again an increase in the number of institutions and scholars in United provinces of Agra and Oudh.

As regarding institutions for female in '1915-16 was 95, in 1916-17 was 111, in 1917-18 was 114, in 1918-19 was 119 and in 1919-20 was 132 regarding secondary schools in these provinces. Figures for female scholars was 9493 in 1915-16, 10,706 in 1916-17, 11,220 in 1917-18, 11,527 in 1918-19 and in 1919-20 was 13,211.'[55] On the basis of these statistical data, there was an increase in both the institutions and in the number of scholars in it. The table given below shows the number of institutions and pupils in United Provinces.

Table 3.17

High schools for girls and their enrollment

Province	Institutions			Pupils		
	1932	1937	Increase	1932	1937	Increase
United Provinces	29	34	5	6354	9691	3337

Source: John Sargent, Progress of Education in India 1932-37.

Above table shows the increased number of institutions and the pupils in the 1932 up to 1937 in United Provinces.

Table 3.18

Middle schools (Anglo-vernacular and vernacular) for girls and their enrolment

Province	Institutions			Pupils		
	1932	1937	Increase(+) Or Decrease(+)	1932	1937	Increase (+) Or Decrease(+)
United Provinces	242	322	+80	33600	49357	+15757

Source: John Sargent., Progress of Education in India 1932-37.

Both the table mentioned above gives the number of institutions and pupils in high stages and middle stages. However, over all in India in fact in all provinces of it before independence a progress can be seen towards in secondary schools. Not satisfactory results came up in United provinces. Progress is very slow as compared to other provinces much more needed to be done in the secondary schools among women for better development.

Provisions of Prizes and Scholarships for Girls

Both prizes and scholarships were created in order to attract more girls towards education system. Prizes or rewards were created in fact for the progress of girls education in the schools, and although act as a source of very great pleasure in their family circles also.

Distribution of prizes especially to girls schools made curious for those family members who were anxious to spread female education. In fact, this is well understood by the native managers or Committees of management of girl's school. However, in many of the different provinces there is a tendency to make formal visit by any officer for the distribution of prizes among girls schools. 'A girl's literature has still to be created in India, and the prizes for girls schools often consist of what are really lesson-books, or even blank copy-books, rather than interesting tales. Many substitutes for books are from time to time adopted, such as pencils, trinkets and above all sweetmeats.'[56] On special occasions, sometime the distribution of clothes was made. All these measures were made to serve public interest in female education. It is hoped that the distribution of suitable books as a suitable measures as a prizes among girls school, will definitely receive the attention of the native association in different parts of India, who are now more interested in the education of their country women.

Another form of reward especially in girl's school to attract more and more girls towards education and to make further progress among them was the provision of scholarships in the different parts of India. It was believed that the scholarship provision for girls than that of boys schools attracted more girls towards education and further more progress could be made in this field. Basically to remove difficulties which creates different kinds of obstacles in the way of women education, in fact the Indian Education Commission recommended the provision of scholarship among women in different stages. The age of scholarships was fixed by the Indian Education Commission especially for those who were above twelve years of age. Mr. Griffith, infact recommends that the 'age limit for candidates for scholarships should be raised by one year, and that the scholarships should be thrown open to girls as well as boys.'[57] In the view of Indian Education Commission, regarding scholarships systems 'adopted in the different provinces to encourage primary education, the commission says that even the despatch of 1854 discuss, that the best pupils of the inferior schools should be provided for by means of scholarships in schools of a higher order, basically not properly carried out in any other province, with the exception of Bengal, as no complete scholarships provision is to be found in any other part of India.'[58] Further the Commission was in the view about scholarships discuss that it basically enable a person to proceed further on from an inferior primary schools to one of the superior one's and in the other words, from a primary school into secondary school. Provision of scholarships mainly differ in different levels. Regarding scholarships, 'the scheme proposed by Govt. prescribe the award for a period of two years of scholarships of Rs. 3 per mensem to encourage women, who have passed the upper primary examination, to read for the vernacular final examinations. Later on it proposed that the scholarships of Rs. 3 per mensem be awarded for two years to encourage women, who have passed the lower primary examinations, to read for the upper primary examination. In different parts of the United Provinces the provisions of scholarships was initiated, like the 'Govt. has accepted an offer made by the Rani Sahiba of Khajurgaon in the Raebaeralli district as to give a sum of Rs. 3000 for poor girls as in the form of scholarships for reading in the girls schools .'[59] It can be said that in different parts of United Provinces like in Raebaerali, Gonda, the provision of scholarships were started. The main aim of this scholarships as to retain more and more girls in the schools and especially for the poor girls and widows who are not eligible to pursue themselves into the higher level. So, this could be the best means to support education system among girls as there was also different provisions of scholarships among women to pursue higher education.

Provision of Curriculum and Text-Books

School education among Indian women, especially in the NWP and Oudh usually understood a means of conferring literacy to the majority of them. Women education was entirely a different ones and therefore it required a special treatment regarding about its general policy. Education for girls basically aims its improvement of their moral and material condition. So, as in the context of education, the two curriculum ie. Curriculum and text-books forms the basic parts in the educational process. There as an absolute unanimity of opinion among all the people regarding the curriculum for girl's school that it should be different from boy's schools. It is stated that the education of girls should be so directed as to fit them about the duties of the home. In fact being wives and mothers as in majority of cases their education will be confirmed to the few years as entering into the household duties. At primary stage the course should be short and simple. Majority of the subjects which should be taught to them should contain all advantages in all primary sections like 'reading, writing, Arithmetic, cutting out and sewing. The optional subjects which may be taught in schools which can make adequate provision for teaching them should be:

1. Clay modeling
2. Kindergarten (paper cutting, pattern making, weaving)
3. Brush work
4. Free hand drawing
5. Recitation of devotional songs
6. Calisthenics

The last two should be taught only in schools where local sentiments would favor their introduction in the school curriculum'[60]. Lower primary section should taught about animals, simple moral stories. Regarding arithmetic, notation, numeration, the four simple rules, multiplication of tables up to 20x10 should be taught in girls schools. As in upper primary section as it should be more advanced and taught subjects on hygiene and sanitation, domestic economy, value of food stuffs, cookery, lives of remarkable men and women and important historical events. In needle works, which should be taught in all classes considered to be most important one as more stress was paid towards it. The above courses are recommended with references to the present state of education in these provinces'[61]. All these courses were implemented in keeping view as the status of education among girls in United Provinces. Basic things and important subjects and lessons were introduced for girls as to provide them the basic knowledge in primary section and further on in higher section it expands.

Regarding text-books for girls the Committee are of opinion that necessary step should be taken on this issue. The language of the primary section should be very simple. Usually the two set of books should be there one for Urdu and one for the Hindi. A more positive step was taken towards the improvement and standardization of text-books.

Provision of Grant-in-Aid Rules for Girls Schools

Apart from the different recommendation of the Indian Committee, grant-in-aid code was also there as to be included in different provinces as a provision for giving help to school managers for the renewal of different necessary measures. ' Grant-in-aid were given with undiscriminating liberality to all promoters of girls school'[62]. As the growth of girls was very slow in these provinces so by introducing grant-in-aid rules by Indian Commission may brought some progress in girls education. The rules for grant-in-aid should be revised in accordance with the recommendation which, however, introduce no changes of importance into our system except: (1) the provision of special scholarships for girls. (2) the establishment of stipendary pupil- teacher-ships, (3) formal recognition of grants for zenana teaching as a proper charge on public funds'[63]. Grant-in-aid rule was one of the important rules made by the Commission for the enhancement of girls education.

In Basti district the report which is submitted by its chairman shows that really appreciable progress has been made on these lines. Not less than 88 aided schools have been opened which teaches up to the upper primary standard. As on 31st March 1897 there were 2,882 puplis on roll, which is more than the satisfactory result. But basically out of these 88 schools no girls attended any of them, the chairman were asked to made enquiry about the proposal which was already made with regard to the govt. schools could not be carried in to effect in these schools also, and girls below a certain age were allowed to attend them'[64]. The system of education in aided schools has been made as far as possible similar to that in use in district board schools. Usually in different parts of India female education is encouraged by giving higher grant rather than from boys schools. But still something more needed to be done to encourage female education in India.

Grants are made to the different institution which actually was a permanently supply of a local want. Different types of grant may be given by the govt. like the maintenance of infrastructure of building etc. later on building grant, equipment grant, maintenance grant was given to the girls school. As model of girls schools was more in very deplorable condition as compared to the boys schools. Less attention was paid towards this. As there was no proper building for the girls school. So different kinds of grant was started to given them. In 1915, there was a special grant for female education by the Govt. of India. As there was a distribution of the Govt. of India's recurring grant of Rs 1,26,000 being the balance available from the grant of Rs 1,40,000 for female education[65]. Therefore, Government of India spends quite money on female education so that a progress could be made in this field. In the year 1906-07, 1907-08, five lakhs rupees were granted for primary education. 'As in 1906-07 on Colleges 1,88,494 Rs were granted, in secondary school Rs 3,24,781 were granted and in primary schools Rs,10,254 were granted. Again in 1907-08 year on colleges Rs 1,55,742 was granted, on secondary school Rs 3,47,998 was granted and on primary school Rs 1,08,422 was granted'[66]. All these figures indicates that grants were given to the different institutions. Later on in 1918 year there was recurring grant by government of India for female education. For the proper growth of female education different funds were made available from different boards like Provincial, Municipal and District boards. Basically by these liberal encouragement of the different agencies shows a genuine interest in the cause of female education.

Basic Scheme of Education

Mahatma Gandhi wrote several articles in Harijan' and shared his views on educational reconstruction in India suggesting a scheme of universal compulsory education for all children of age group of 6-13 years through the medium of their mother-tongue which lead them of their all round development of the person. At primary schools they should be taught like processing of cotton, wool and silk, paper making and cutting, book binding etc. which could serve a double purpose for them.

In October 1937, the National Education Conference held under the president ship of Gandhi which resolved that: (1) free and compulsory education should be provided for seven years on a nation-wide scale, (2) the medium of instruction should be the mother-tongue, (3) the process of education should centre round some form of manual productive work, (4) all the facilities of the child be developed by being integrally related to the central handicraft, (5) the system of education should gradually be able to cover the remuneration of teachers. The conference then appointed a committee for framing a syllabus for Basic schools.[67] In provincial governments run by the congress started introducing the Wardha scheme from 1938. In 1939, Govt. of United Provinces, Assam, Orissa and Bombay had initiated some steps, but the other provinces did not introduce the scheme. They faced little bit problem like the non-availability of actual funds, not having proper trained teachers, new text-books. Overall Gandhi's basic education wanted to lay the foundation of a common citizenship, and an overall development of an individual.

Post War Plan of Educational Developments

In the year 1944, Sir John Sargent, the then Education Advisor with the government of India asked to prepare a memorandum on post war educational development in India. The report is popularly known as Sargent report, entitled post-war educational development in India. The main motto of the plan was to create in India, in a period of not less than 40 years, the same standards of educational attainments as had already been attained in England. The report also recommended about the provision of pre-primary education for children of 3 and 6 years, also recommend about the provision of universal free and compulsory education for all children from 6 to 14 years, also higher education for selected children, and also for technical, commercial and art education.

By 1947, 'when the British power was withdrawn from India, educational opportunities had been opened to women at all stages and their social status had been raised to some extent. This type of education basically creates a new awareness among people and opened a new way of life to them.'[68] Next chapter, discusses the role of Christian Missionaries in opening educational institutions and their efforts in the development female education.

FOOTNOTES

1. N.L. Gupta, *Women Education through the Ages,* Concept Publishing Company, New Delhi, p.107
2. Ibid, p. 24.
3. Ibid, p. 107
4. Y.B. Mathur, *Women's Education in India*, Asia Publishing House, Bombay 1973., pp 5-6.
5. Ibid, p.6
6. S. Bandopadhyay, *From Plassey to Partition*, Orient BlackSwan New Delhi, 2013, p.142.
7. S.C. Ghosh, *The History Of Education in Modern India 1757-2012*, Orient BlackSwan New Delhi, 2013, p.103
8. Y.B. Mathur, *Women's Education in India 1813-1966,* Asia Publishing House, Bombay, 1973 .,p7.
9. S.C. Ghosh, *The History of Education in Modern India 1757-2012*, Orient BlackSwan New Delhi, 2013, p.80.
10. N.L. Gupta, *Women Education through the Ages,* Concept Publishing Company, New Delhi. 2000, p.109.
11. S. Bhattacharya, *The Development of Women's Education in India.*,p.31.
12 Y.B. Mathur, *Women's Education in India, 1813-1966,* Asia Publishing House, Bombay, 1973, p.,28.
13. S.C., Ghosh, *The History of Education in Modern India, 1757-2012*, Orient BlackSwan New Delhi, 2013, p.81.
14. N.L. Gupta, *Women Education through the Ages*, Concept Publishing Company, New Delhi, 2000., p.109.
15. Document no.22, A.P. Howell note on "Education in British India, 1870-71, S. Bhattacharya (ed.), *The Development of Women's Education in India, A Collection of Documents 1850-1920*, Kanishka Publishers, Distributors, New Delhi., p.55.
16. Ibid, p.58.
17 Ibid., p.61.

18. Ibid., p.65.
19. R.T.H. Griffith, Report on the Progress of Education in N.W.P and Oudh for the year 1875-76, Allahabad, N.W.P. Govt. Press, 1876.
20. Report on Public Instruction in the N.W.P and Oudh for 1877-78, Allahabad, Govt. Press., p.70.
21. Ibid., p. 73
22. Ibid., p. 73
23. S. Bhattacharya, The Development of Women's Education, p.119.
24. S.C. Ghosh, *The History of Education in Modern India 1757-2012,* Orient BlackSwan New Delhi, 2013., p.92.
25. File no, 3/1884, Education Department, Report of the Indian Education Commission, Education Deptt.
26. Ibid, p.81.
27. Lyall, A.C. (1835-1911); entered service in Bengal in 1855; served in the western regions of NWP, 1856-73; held various officers as secretary to the government of India, Home and Foreign department; Lt. Governor of NWP and Oudh. 1882-87; Chancellor of Allahabad University and member of Indian council 1883-1903.
28. File no. 3/1884, Education Department, Report of the Indian Education Commission.
29. Ibid., p. 57
30. Ibid., p.49.
31. File no. 3/1884, Education Department, Report of the Indian Education Commission, p.159.
32. A.M. Nash, Progress of Education in India 1887-88 to 1891-92, Second Quinquennial Review,. p. 294.
33. R. Nathan, Progress of Education in India 1897-98 to 1901-02, Fourth Quinquennial Review, 1904 published.
34. J.S. Cotton, Progress of Education in India 1892-93 to 1896-97, Third Quinquennial Review, p.307.
35. John Sargent, Progress of Education in India 1932-37, 11th Quinquennial Review, p.157, Vol.1, 1940, Delhi.
36. File no.762 of 1923, Complusory Primary Education in Sitapur Municipality, Education Deptt.

37. File no. 979 of 1921, Complusory Primary Education in Cawnpore Municipality, Education Deptt.
38. File no.1020 of 1925, United Provinces District Boards Primary Education Act 1926, Education Deptt.
39. File no.1136 of 1935, Compulsory Primary Education for Girls in Cawnpore Municipality, Education Deptt.
40. Ibid.
41. File no. 1025 of 1933, Resolution by Mrs. Kailash Srivastava regarding girls compulsory Education, Education Department .There are some major resolution which took up by Mrs. Kailash Srivastava regarding girls compulsory education. As in resolution 12 of their first meeting held at Cawnpore on Jan 18, 1932, the Girls Education Inquiry Committee suggested that opinion be invited from municipalities, where compulsory education for boys has already been introduced, in regard to the possibility of introducing it for girls. The no. of girls in school is small compared with the no. of boys. On resolution no. 5 o their second meeting held at Lucknow on Nov 20,1932,the Girls Education Inquiry Committee, while considering the advisability of introducing compulsory education should be controlled by the Govt. and that the experiment should be tried in urban areas. To obtain funds it suggested that the house tax be increased by 2 piece or one anna per rupee as necessary and the money thus obtained be earmarked for girls education.
42. Ibid.
43. File no. 1063 of 1936, Compulsory Primary Education for Girls in Itaunja and Kakori village areas., Education Department,
44. File no. 1025 of 1933, Resolution by Mrs. Kailash Srivastava regarding girls compulsory education, Education Department.
45. Ibid.
46. Ibid.
47. J.S. Cotton, Progress of Education in India 1892 to 1897.
48. M.S. Sundaram, *Education in British India*, The Journal of Negro Education., Vol. 15,1946. Accessed on 15/1/2016
49. Y.B. Mathur, *Women's Education in India*, p.84.
50. S.Bhattacharya, *The Development of Women's Education in India*: A Collection of Documents 1850-1920, Kanishk Publishers, New Delhi., p.221.

51. A.M. Nash, Progress of Education in India 1887-88 to 1891-92.
52. J.S. Cotton, Progress of Education in India, 1892-93 to 1896-97.
53. Deptt. of Statistics India, Statistical abstract for British India, Vol v Education, 1913-14, Calcutta, 1915.
54. Deptt. of Statistical India, Statistics of British India. Vol v Education 1915-16, Calcutta, 1917.
55. Deptt. of Statistical India, Statistics of British India. Vol v Education 1919-20, Calcutta, 1921.
56. S. Bhattacharya, *The Development of Women's Education in India A collection of Documents 1850-1920,* Kanishka Publishers, New Delhi, p.150.
57. File no. 40, Code of regulations for European schools, NWP and Oudh, 1884, Education Deptt., NWP and Oudh.
58. File no. 3/1884, Report of the Indian education Commission, Education Deptt.
59. File no. 177 of 1909, Lady Hewett Scholarship Endowment Trust, Rae Baerali, United Provinces, Education Dept.
60. File no. 332A/ 11 of 1905, Report of the Committee on Female Education United Provinces, Education Deptt.
61. Ibid.
62. File no. 3/1884, Report of the Indian Education Commission, Education Deptt.
63. Ibid.
64. File no. 81, Grant-in-aid to Vernacular Primary Schools in NWP and Oudh, Education Deptt.
65. File no. 4/ 1915, Govt. of India's special grant for female education, Education Deptt.
66. File 119 of 1908, Five lakhs grant for University Education, Education Deptt.
67. Y.B. Mathur, *Women's Education in India* 1813-1966, Asia Publishing House, Bombay, 1973., p.93.
68. Ibid, p.103.

5

Role of Christian Institutions Regarding Women Education

Indian education system was one of the old system in the world. But watershed took place only under the colonial government. The British made several kinds of experiments in the field of education. At the beginning of the nineteenth century, when missionaries came in to the forefront in India then it totally gave a push factor in the wheel of social change in the country. As a result by the turn of the century Indian society had taken a long stride ahead. Basically, the missionaries in India represented not only a new religion in front of Indian people but also a new way of life. They made lot of efforts by their methods of propagation in the field of education, medical, charity and last but not least in maintaining the lost status of women in the society and to avail them the opportunities of education and by prohibiting the certain different issues related to women. As earlier by the methods of their propagation very few persons of the elite classes were attracted towards this new religion. But later on the depressed classes of the society who were discriminated by the upper castes of the society were mainly influenced by the teaching methods of the Christian missionaries. They could see a ray of new hope and also for a better life by establishing religious affinity with the ruling race. Mostly people from depressed classes got converted in to the Christianity religion as it does not discriminate the people and they can have a new identity and respect in the society. Christian missionaries generally don't discriminate people on any grounds. They treated people equally earlier when Christian missionaries landed in India they want to convert people of India in to Christian, but later on undoubtedly they worked truly in the different fields of society like to improve the education, in the field of medical without any biasness in their mind of conversion thought. Their works mostly shows their dedication in the services of people.

Christianity was not a certain new religion in India during nineteenth century only. Christianly entered Indian soil when one of the Apostels of Jesus came to the Southern coast of India. But it was confined up to the Southern parts of the country. Except a few pockets of Roman Catholics and the Serampore missionaries near Calcutta, it was almost an unknown faith in Northern India.

Education during British Period

It is a very well known fact that education is an essential and a basic need of human beings in today's life scenario and same it was the concept in earlier time. But in earlier time with the advent of the British in the administration of Indian system brings totally changes in the society. Different kinds of educational institutes were developed during British period. The British did not pay very much attention towards the education of Indians. Earlier they started only such kind of education which could provide them best clerks for their administration. So, they did not do much in this field. Their education system only benefitted limited persons of the Indian society. It remains mostly untouched by the lower strata of the society. Before coming on the British India was a very cultured society. As women were very much respected in the society and were educated too. But after the advent of the British and the establishment of their different colonies in India mainly draw their less attention towards the degraded condition of women. They were least interested in this field. They lost their right over education and also were subjected towards the social evils of the Indian society.

Now, the question arises that what was the nature of this Indian education system when the British came to India? From the different sources, and from the writings of different historians the Indian education system as of the Vedic age was based on spiritual and classical rather than of practical in nature. Mainly emphasis was on the classical languages of the Hindus and the Muslims, as in Sanskrit, Arabic respectively. A general idea of everything related to day to day life was imparted to the scholars. As there were Pathsalas and Maktabs and for this Gurus and the Maulavis were appointed to impart education. Girls also were educated in institutions and at home. Culture of educating girls was there in ancient times.

As these kinds of practices were lost with the advent of the British in India, the British or The East India Company (EIC) got the Diwani in 1765.[1] This established the footprints of the British in India as to rule over it and to run the administration of India. The British were least interested in the educational policy towards India. They did not took up so much of effort in maintaining the educational status of both men and women. Apart from the few official of EIC like William Jones, Jonathan Duncan the resident of Benaras in 1792 did a lot to preserve the ancient learning and literature of India by their works. So, it can be said very few officials of EIC were interested in promoting ancient Indian learning. William Jones, was well known by establishing the 'Asiatic society' of Bengal on 15th January 1784, with its aim as to give a great filip to ancient learning in India. As Jones, himself developed a great taste of Sanskrit learning as well as, Jonathan Duncan, who was the resident of Benaras shows his interests in preserving the ancient laws, literature and scriptures of the Hindus by establishing a Sanskrit college at Benaras.[2]

Later on few British officials who worked for the up-liftment of women status by sharing their views to supress the different evils like Sati, female infanticide, Thughee etc. Their support really helped women somehow in maintaining their status, no doubt but very little. So, very few amount of work was done from the British.

Charter Act of 1813 and Missionaries Intervention in India

The Charter Act of 1813 was a landmark in the history of education in context of India. Without the 1813 charter, the discussion of history of education was incomplete. To improve the Indian education system, a clause was inserted in the East India Company's Act of

1813, that Governor-General had to denote not less than one lakh of rupees annually to education. This was the first time it happened that some amount of rupees was fixed and made compulsory to spend on education. It was the first time that in 1813 that the EIC accepted the responsibility towards the education.[3] This Act also played an important role in the intervention of Missionaries towards the different corners of India. Charter of 1813 opened a gate for the CIA to enter in to the field of Indian education and worked in this field. Charter Act of 1813 merely compelled the EIC to accept the responsibility for the education of the Indian people.

Missionaries Enterprises in India

As mentioned above that Charter Act of 1813 opened a gate of India to welcome the Missionaries societies. From 1813 onwards basically a new era of missionaries activities began in India. The various missionaries societies started their missions in different parts of the India including United Provinces. Some of them are the General Baptist Missionary Society, the London Missionary Society, the Church Missionary Society, the Wesleyan Mission and the Scotch Missionary Society[4], started their educational instructions in different sections of India.

There are general causes which generally propagated the works of Missionaries in India. Firstly, it could be noticed that imparting education was never the main object of the missionaries, they just want to train up the Indians assistants mainly for their proselytizing activities. Secondly, it can be said that, the Missionaries made lot of efforts to raise the lower class of the society who were very depressed and could not understand any other language. So, missionaries promoted the Vernacular languages. Thirdly, missionaries did effortless work in promoting the education among women. As it was considered the most "dangerous" area in which they took up the stand. Different missionary women workers began to educate the girls and women by opening day schools for Indian girls and by Zenana system of education and also by opening the Orphan homes for women.[5] These work are the really milestone works by the by the missionaries which raised the status of India and of women also, slowly but progressive. Another great change which was brought up by missionaries was the introduction of English languages through their instruction. Result was that lot of people earlier joined mission schools for the sake of learning English languages, Western knowledge and these later on effected the higher classes of the society. The result was that mission school exercised a greater influence over the government schools, and also their thoughts effected the old Indians thoughts especially in context of girls status. Later on different schools and colleges were founded in United Provinces as for example in 1853, the Church Missionary Society founded St. John's College at Agra.

Christian Missionaries and Women Education in United Provinces

The Christian Missionaries played an important and vital role in the development of education in India. Apart from this they are the pioneer one's who helped in promoting female education in different parts of India. They are the actual initiators in the field of education during colonial India. It was for the first time in 1813 that the East India Company accepted the responsibility for the education of the people. As it restricted its educational activities to men and even refused not to do any kind of action towards the education of girls and women. They totally neglected it and did not pay any kind of attention. Simply the reason assume that the deeply so called the social customs and prejudice that bound them to take any kind of education. The company, therefore, refused to grant any financial assistance for the establishment of girls school.[6] Some more new kinds of work need to be done in the attitude of women education. No doubt, missionaries played the role of pioneers in this field. They were the earliest one who played attention towards this field. Actually, there was a general thinking almost among various missionaries societies that through education only that they influence the people of India, especially the lower class people and women who were deprived away from all opportunities. In fact, education was considered as the cause and end of proselytization. Most of them is of the view that education alone would help in developing the personality of women. As western education would enlighten them to get rid away from the different kinds of social evils that were prevailing in the societies. Apart from the education they would provide the basic essential things to mould the character of the child.

As mentioned above, Christianity to spread as a religion was the main intention of the early missionaries. As during the year 1870s, this approach was failed by the Indian Brahmans and the other high caste people because they were receiving the education without any restriction. Then later on they focused on women and lower caste people who were mainly deprived from their basic rights, as to spread their religion and knowledge. By the time, the Church Missionary Society (CMS), the London Missionary Society (LMS), the Society for the Propagation of the Gospel (SPG) and the Cambridge Mission to Delhi (CMD) were the mostly missionaries societies who involved in teaching in no. of high schools and colleges across the major portion of North India. Even the societies who involved in education in NWP of Agra and Oudh (later United Provinces) were the CMS, LMS and SPG. These were highly active in the field of education. India's most populous province, in United Provinces these missionary societies ran over half of the high schools and also different colleges. American missionary societies, in contrast, worked overwhelmingly with the lower caste communities and were less involved themselves in higher levels of education. On the other hand, Anglican mission schools interacted more with the vast number of groups and communities who would go on to lead the Indian nationalist movement.'[7]

Basically, the missionary activities started with the formation of the major missionary societies like Baptist Missionary Society (1792), the London Missionary Society (1799), the Church Missionary Society (1799), the American Board of Commissioners for foreign missions (1810), the Methodist missionary society (1813). When on November 11, 1793 William Carey[8] arrived in India which was considered to be the starting point of this phase of missionary activities. One of the pioneer of the Baptist Missionary, William Carey, laid great importance to education and believed that schools were one of the most effectual means of spreading the light of the gospel through the world. Later on in 1830, the convention of missionary schools was further strengthened by Alexander Duff, a Scottish Presbyterian missionary done a great job. He laid the downward filtration policy concept and introduced English language as a medium of instruction in his schools instead of Vernacular or local languages. After the Charter Act of 1813, Wood's Education

Despatch of 1854, somehow encouraged the missionaries to enter in to the field of education. The Despatch suggested the government's gradual withdrawal from, the field of education in favour of some private educational agency. This withdrawal of government filled the missionaries with new hope and also presenting themselves as a substitute for the government in the field of education. Some grant-in-aid scheme also provided them, which later on helped them to uphold their strong position in the education system. From 1850 onwards, education department was set up by the government to look after education. By the time the missionaries educational institutions expands themselves as their network also not only in U.P. but also in major portion of India also. The missionaries, with the help of their other communities of the society, made good efforts for the education of girls in United Provinces. This period till up to the dawn of the twentieth century, could be called as the period of transition for the missionaries, because they themselves are busy in outlining their future course of action.

As in 1882-83, recommendations by the first Indian Education Commission showed little interest for the missionaries. It also recommended the grant of financial support for the native private agencies, through the scheme of grant-in-aid to native private agencies. Grant-in-aid system helped them financially and to do their work more effectively. Missions schools improved the standard of instruction in the schools and in colleges and also catch the attention of the upper echelon of the society. Most of the people now started sending their children to the missionary schools. They usually draw to the missionary institutions due to the higher standards of education system which was maintained by the missionary educators at these institutions. It can be said that now this was the time period when the missionaries almost leading the race by their efforts and finally emerged as the symbol of excellence in the province with its great efforts towards the education and especially among women.

Present education system of the United Province is the legacy of the colonial education system. Although the CM (Christian Missionaries) was one of the important players in developing this kind of education system in the United Province which is still functioning in some modified form. Imparting education has been the most striking features about the missionary strategy and especially among women.

There is no doubt that in United Provinces the cause of female education was taken up by the missionaries. They did a lot of work not only in United Provinces but also in major parts of India. They invoked the people of India of the different benefits by educating women in their family. Apart from the proselytism, which was their main aim, imparting education to women became their main motto. As this was the danger area to enter but then also they were successful in this area. Besides opening up different schools in United Provinces they played an important part in preparation, publication and distribution of text-books and also reading material for women. As mentioned earlier in the chapter that the missionaries basically run their methods of education through three agencies:

1. by the arrangement of day schools for girls which was mainly attended by the Hindu poorer classes or by low people.
2. by establishing orphanages, who were mainly converted to Christianity.
3. and last but most important agency to impart education i.e. Zenana system for Hindu ladies and Muslim ladies.

As these above mentioned schools were mostly financed by the private resources of the individual missionary, his society in England or America and secondly also by the system of grant-in-aid from the government. There were very few govt. schools in Oudh region but later on during 1865-66 there were 10 schools for the native girls which were managed by the missionaries bodies, and among them five are connected with the church of England and five are connected with the American mission.'[9] As respecting them the director of public instruction mainly wrote that, 'the schools are regularly visited by the two missionary ladies who really express their views in the favour about the progress which was made by the pupils of Oudh. Mainly instructions were given in reading, writing and arithmetic like subjects.'[10] Again the same report the next views are that, He mentions that Mr. Reuther of Fyzabad, has opened nearly about one or two girl's school in this city. The Head

Masters of some of the Zillah and Tehsil schools during the past year showed their interests in the favor about the progress in female education in the city and some 2 or 3 small schools were also opened, but their success was not too much.[11] Although from the above report of the DIP of Oudh schools clearly during the expansion of time period the missionaries took up interest in female education in the provinces and by watching the same effort some more schools were opened by other officials. People now became more active in promoting female education in the provinces.

By the efforts of missionaries, now different schools were opened by the people in different sections of the United Provinces. With the coming of years different schools were opened by the missionaries in Agra, Allahabad, Benaras etc. During 1862, six mission schools were opened by the missionaries, later on soon followed by Bareilly, Etawah, Fatehpur and Allahabad had different mission schools especially for girls. Different types of grant-in-aid system helped in promoting female education. The American mission and the Church mission societies mainly reported about the creditable success of their pupils including elderly ladies from different respectable families both from the Hindus and the Muslims. Mostly their schools were spread at Lucknow, Fayzabad, Unnao, Bahraich, Sultanpur Hardoi in all other districts of the provinces. Table 4.1 as given below shows the number of institutions and attendance of girls in private schools during the year 1869 to 1871.

Table 4.1

Private female schools aided

Years		**No. of Institutions**	**No. of pupils on roll at the close of the year**	**Average attendance during the year**
Middle class girl's schools	1869-70	1	80	40
	1870-71	1	71	53
Lower class girl's schools	1869-70	10	291	193
	1870-71	15	316	257

Source: S. Bhattacharya, The Development of Women's Education in India: A Collection of Documents 1850-1920., p.60

As above table clearly shows that the no. of institutions of girls during the year of 1869 up to 1870 and also no. of pupils and the average attendance in these institutions. Out of these schools as five schools belongs to the Anglican Church Mission and eight to the American Methodist Mission. It is generally said that girls are not equal in these institutions as compared to the government pupils.[12] The works of missionaries were incredible in the field of female education. They were pioneer in this field. Earlier even the Wood' Despatch of 1854 found 17 Missionary girl's schools along with 386 pupils in the North-Western Provinces and Oudh. So, their efforts are countless. The early efforts of the missionaries were almost succeeded on the part of the Education Department. Later on the part of missionaries the education system grows and met with success in some of the district and in some of the districts met with the failure. Time and again missionaries were also extending their operations in different districts of United Provinces for the promotion of female education. Girls schools are being established by the govt. and by the missionaries as to promote female education. Missionary effort has been steadily directed for so many years to the education of Christian and non-Christian girls. No doubt the standard of education is generally low in United Provinces as compared to other provinces, as on one hand the people generally don't send their daughter due to fear to convert in to Christianity and next, the so called evil or social customs that was going on in every provinces. But in spite of all these challenges the missions continued to do their work without any fear. During the year of 1885-86, there are 22 high and middle schools, in which 13 are of Europeans and Eurasians and the rest are chiefly from Native Christians. Mr. Nesfield, find education was almost stationary in the aided schools and most of the girls are learning different things.

Another view of Mr. Nesfield about the education in NWP was that, if some of the real work was done in context of education then it is only in the schools of the Anglo-Vernacular class, and in few missionary middle schools for Christian girls.[13] Higher education of women mainly depended on mission schools and each school receives grant-in-aid from the private enterprises, to maintain its efficiency.

Mission schools are making their efforts to promote education and more schools at primary, secondary and at higher level. During the year of 1887-88, 163 primary schools are there for native girls which were maintained by District and Municipal boards against 168 in the previous year 3694 were total people that were mainly enrolled. The figures are not encouraging, and the District Boards which have closed schools of this class after a long experience of failure cannot be blamed. Basically, the figures of aided girls schools are more encouraging. Almost 167 schools educate nearly about 6600 girls. 9 of these schools teach up to the secondary level. Mostly these are the outcome of the missionary effort, and the testimony borne by the Director of Public Instruction to the work done by the missionary societies in the education of native girls is amply justified.'[14] With the coming days the result about the girls education are satisfactory by the different reports of the Inspector of the Institutions.

J.S. Cotton also highlights the progress of women education in his report of the year for 1892-97, and briefly describes the achievements of the Govt. up to 1896 and the role played by different agencies and associations since 1898. J.S. Cotton clearly describes the growth of women education in NWP and Oudh provinces. He argues that, 'during from last five years the total no. of schools for Indian girls has steadily fallen from 320 to 227 or nearly about 13 percent of the decrease was there in almost under the head of Aided or Unaided primary schools. No. of pupils also fell down, but gradually improvement took place and for the entire period the no. has risen from 8729 to 10502 or nearly by 8 percent. Similarly, in the context to secondary level it shows a pretty advance from 145 to 237. Increase can also be seen in Anglo-Vernacular schools for girls from 17 to 25, in which 18 are as secondary and 7 as primary. He also argues that no explanation is given for the fact that why girls aided schools needs more funds than a board schools'.[15] As noticed that girls school needs more attention and money as compared to the boys schools.

Another person called L.M. Thornton, in his report on women education in the NWP and Oudh clearly gives perfect explanation about education and also gives comments on progress of women's education also points out the various hindrances in the way towards it. He is of the view that there has been satisfactory increased in context of girls schools in the provinces and also in the no. of scholars that attending the schools during the year. There was an increase in the no. of girls reading in primary schools for boys during this year mainly from 471 to 2670. Increment mainly occurred chiefly in the schools of the Fayzabad divisions, nearly about 1565 girls'.[16] The table given below gives the no. of schools and scholars in Anglo-Vernacular schools and data on no. of colleges for girls.

Table 4.2

Anglo-Vernacular schools and colleges for girls

Class of Institution	Year	Number of Scholars					
		No. of schools	In college classes	In high stages	In middle stage	In primary stage	Total
Colleges	1899-1900	1	17	-	-	-	17
	1898-99	1	21	-	-	-	21
Secondary schools	1899-1900	18	-	40	192	1501	1733
	1898-99	18	-	31	203	1495	1729
Primary schools	1899-1900	9	-	-	-	496	496
	1898-99	11	-	-	-	913	913
Total	1899-1900	28	17	40	192	1997	2246
	1898-99	30	21	31	203	2408	2663

Source: S. Bhattacharya, The Development of Women's Education in India: A Collection of Documents 1850-1920., p.302.

These schools which are mentioned in the above table are almost without exception maintained by missionary societies. In Lucknow, there is college called women's college on which American Methodists Episcopal Missions spent large amount of money. Above table shows little variations in the enrolments of girls in secondary stages, but as compared to primary stages it has decreased considerably. Satisfactory work was done by the Managers of the London Mission Orphanage of Mirzapur. As report of the Inspectress reveals from this school that these Mission doing efforts to educate famine children which deserve special mention.Table mentioned below gives the statistics about the Primary Vernacular schools for girls mostly aided schools.

Table 4.3

Primary Vernacular schools for Girls and Aided Schools

Division	Year	No. of schools	Number of Scholars		
			Upper Primary	Lower Primary	Total
Agra	1899-1900	20	25	710	735
	1898-99	15	6	575	581
Bundelkhand	1899-1900	1	-	17	17
	1898-99	1	-	19	19
Lucknow	1899-1900	14	89	705	794
	1898-99	13	88	592	680
Fyzabad	1899-1900	8	15	230	245
	1898-99	8	-	251	251
Allahabad	1899-1900	6	2	259	261
	1898-99	7	11	393	404
Benaras	1899-1900	41	21	1951	1972
	1898-99	37	195	1912	2107
Rohilkhand	1899-1900	49	27	1365	1392
	1898-99	41	-	1043	1043
Meerut	1899-1900	22	24	746	770
	1898-99	20	20	746	766
Kumaun	1899-1900	4	-	137	137
	1898-99	3	-	123	123
Total	1899-1900	165	203	6120	6323
	1898-99	145	320	5654	5974

Source: S. Bhattacharya, The Development of Women's Education in India: A Collection of Documents 1850-1920., p.306.

The figures of aided Vernacular primary schools (as mentioned in above table) are satisfactory when compared with previous year. As no. of schools and scholars are found increasing and support could be seen from municipal boards who contribute a lot for female education. It means they are taking a lot of interest in promoting female education. Most of the important thing is that these schools are managed by the majority of missionaries. Statistics revealed that no. of schools and no. of female schools are more in aided schools which are mostly run by missionaries as compared with the no. of schools and no. of female scholars in the schools under Public management, which are mostly run by the govt. This reveals that missionaries are doing more efforts in promoting female scholars towards their institutions.

Report of Robert Nathan of 1904, reveals that a beginning was made by the different missionaries societies for the promotion of female education, as well as they throughout played an important part in the diffusion of knowledge among the people of India of the benefits of having educated women in our country. Most of the Primary, Secondary and Higher education were maintained by the missionary societies. Among secondary schools in the year of 1904, there were 38 institutes which managed by missionary.'[17] Most of the private schools belonged to missionary societies. In context of this the Director of the United Provinces says that, most of the aided schools are chiefly managed by the missionary societies. Among non-missionary schools, the City school of Allahabad, is the only one that can properly be said to thrive.'[18] In context of collegiate education there was the increase by five colleges in United Provinces in the year of 1896-97. The list includes the Isabella Thoburn college at Lucknow, and five Europeans and Eurasian girls schools along with college departments. Among this one is at Allahabad and the rest are in the hills.

Apart from the growth in primary and in secondary schools, missionaries were making growth in Collegiate education among women. So, that they can move forward in life and could get higher education in their life. In 1870, the opening of Isabella Thoburn College[19] in Lucknow created history in United Provinces, as it was the most of the populous college opened and maintained by the missionaries which attracted many girls and example can be seen with the growth in the no. of female students in the college. With the passage of time, there was bulk of female secondary and higher education institutes maintained by missionaries. Account of women's education is incomplete without the description of the Isabella Thoburn College which is one of the largest and popular college in context of higher education to girls in Northern India. With the coming years there was the growth in different schools and colleges which were established by the missionary societies. During the year of 1899-1900, there was growth in the no. of scholars in Anglo-Vernacular Institutions which was nearly almost maintained by missionary societies, and also an increment could be seen in the aided primary schools for girls from 445 with 5974 pupils to 165 with 6323 pupils.'[20] So, increased no. of schools can be seen in these mission societies. A good progress can be seen in different colleges in different districts of United Provinces. In 1902, there were now eight aided college, and grant-in-aid has been sanctioned during the year to 97 colleges for women in Lucknow.'[21] In context of Secondary Anglo-Vernacular schools, it was up to twenty and being two more than in the year of 1902.[22] Again in the year of 1911-12, excellent work was done in the IT College at Lucknow, as last year its enrolment was 30 in the college.[23] With the coming of the days now there is a gradual desire of education of girls as well as education to more girls. The IT College had a larger building as it got help from women's foreign missionary society of the Methodist Episcopal Church which relieved the colleges of debt of over four lakhs.[24] IT College was the college where scholars from different other provinces attend the college as to receive education. Moreover, this college is not restricted to the education of Indian women, but others like European students are also permitted to receive higher education.[25] Another one namely, The Women's College of Lucknow is supported by the Women's missionary society of the Methodist Episcopal Church of America. As it was affiliated to the Allahabad University up to B.A. degree, as students were enrolled every year.[26] No doubt, that this college occupies an important place in the educational field.

Table 4.4

Figures of Govt. schools and missionary schools in U.P. during the year 1912

Schools	**Govt. schools**	**Mission run and aided**
Colleges	9	38
High schools	59	248
Primary	6018	4350

Source: Hayden J.A. Bellenoit, Missionary Education and Empire in Late Colonial India, 1860-1920, p.51

As these statistics reveal that government schools as compared with mission-run aided schools was low. No. of colleges was higher in mission-run and in aided schools as compared to government schools. And finally the no. of primary schools are more in govt. schools in contrast to mission-run aided schools. Next, table given below gives the figures about no. of recognized schools in India during the year of 1910-11.

Table 4.5

Recognized schools in India, 1910-11

	Government	**Missions**	**Total**
Art colleges	28	53	136
2nd schools	740	1785	3285
Primary	24715	5194	112930

Source: Hayden J.A. Bellenoit, Missionary Education and Empire in Late Colonial India, 1860-1920,p.51.

Above table gives the clear no. of govt. art colleges and primary schools in contrast to mission schools. As Art colleges are more in no. in mission as compared to govt. schools. And in secondary schools also the missions came with more no. of schools as compared to govt. schools. And in secondary schools also the missions came with more no. of schools as compared to govt. schools. As well as in primary schools, the no. were more in govt. than in missions. So, in nutshell, it can be said that apart from the govt. success also, the missions also doing their best to improve the education at different stages. At Benaras also, the Church Missionary society was doing excellent work by having a boarding school for Christian girls with 100 pupils around.[27] Table listed below give no. of schools for Indian girls of United Provinces some under Public Management and some under Private Management.

Table 4.6

Schools for Indian Girls in the United Provinces

Under Public Management				Under Private Management	
Government		Local or Municipal branch	Native states	Aided	Unaided
High schools	-	-	-	6	-
Middle English	-	1	-	18	4
Vernacular	-	-	-	7	-
Primary	57	355	-	499	17
Training schools	1	-	-	7	3
Total	58	356	-	537	24

Source: Public Instruction Report for United Provinces, 1910, from Minna G. Cowan, The Education of the Women of India–Primary source edition, p.132.

Above table clearly mention all figures related to no. of schools for Indian girls under govt., local or Municipal, native states, aided and unaided also. And a vast differences can be seen between these schools and majority schools are run by missionaries, as most of the aided schools are run by missions. So, from the all different sources it revealed that missionaries are successful in operating a large no. of schools for girls in United Provinces.

Zenana Teaching

The word 'Zenana' means simply a mode of instruction of females in their own houses by visiting teachers. Due to the different obstacles in the progress of women education not only in Oudh region, but in whole of India certain initiatives needed. To get rid from the different social prejudices, some changes were necessary. Zenana teaching was one of the necessities of the time and it was mostly carried out by the female missionaries. So, the entrance of female missionaries in to the picture was more important, as to achieve the missionary objectives. Because the male missionaries were denied the access of native female population, which means about nearly almost half of the population remained out of their influence. So, there is a great need of female missionaries. For this largest missionary societies like the society for the propagation of the Gospel, the Church missionary society, the London Missionary society, committees recruit lady missionaries during the 19th century.

The most successful efforts yet made to educate Indian women after leaving school was only due to missionaries. Not only in Oudh, in fact in all provinces of India, lady missionaries took zeal to educate native ladies both of Hindus and Muslim of India, at their home. Their instruction is confined to the female members only of the family and they also taught Christianity along with the secular subjects. Almost in every case, study of secular subjects was a part of the schemes.

Women missionaries occupy the activity of 'Zenana visiting' in different provinces. Moreover, most of the lady missionaries believed that women and girls of the Oudh provinces could not attend schools due to larger role in domestic household. Consequently, the missionaries established a regular system of visiting the homes and impart them education to native ladies of the provinces. The women missionaries were suppressed to effect religious and up to some level the social change in the provinces through their mode of instructions which they usually gave.

The female missionaries responded very positively in the society and also contributed significantly for the betterment of the women of the United Provinces. The lady missionaries devoted their lives for the cause of female education in the U.P through the mode of home-teaching in the native families then willingly. These Zenana visiting groups mainly composed of one or more European ladies along with the trained staff of Native Christians or Anglo-Indian young women, who taught in the Zenanas allotted to them.'[28] In 1882 the Hunter Commission especially looked in to the possibilities of encouraging more private enterprise. Result was that commission highly appreciated the missionary agency i.e. The Zenana teaching.

From 1860 onwards, different women's societies from England, Germany and some from America entered in India. Apart from women missionaries, the wives and daughters of the missionaries too involved in the promotion of female education in different provinces of India. By these missionaries a communication barrier was broken between Indian and Western woman, and a sharing bond was established by sharing knowledge. Although the contacts were but the results were far, wider and deeper.

Zenana instruction was imposed in different districts of U.P like Lucknow, Etawah, Kanpur, Mainpuri, Benaras etc. And positive results came out from these instructions. Even the Department of Education appreciated the missionaries way of work as it brought positive result in context of female education. Most of the female educational efforts were more importantly directed towards Zenana system of education, which resulted in substantial growth during the later of nineteenth century in the provinces. Here, are the list of some of the societies who took up the cause for the Zenana teaching:

1. The American Presbyterian Mission
2. The Women's Missionary Society of America
3. Church of England Zenana Mission Society for the promotion of female education normally in the East
4. Indian female normal schools
5. Women's Foreign missionary society of the Methodist Episcopal Church
6. The Church of Scotland Ladies society for female Education
7. Women's Union Missionary Society of America
8. The Zenana Bible and Medical Mission World Women's Christian Temperance Union.

So, these are different societies mainly of women missionaries who worked for the promotion of female education in different parts of the India. However, in 1870, a good work reported at Benaras of Zenana teachings. Later on with the passage of time most of the Zenana instruction was carried out in several other districts of United Provinces like in Kanpur, Farrukhabad, Bareilly, Allahabad, Fatehgarh and in Lucknow also. It is clear from the different reports and from different records that dept. of education and the govt. remained in favor towards the Zenana missions. With the large reduction in no. of govt. schools and consequently the financial crisis lead the Zenana mission to hold its position in different parts of the India. However, the Hunter Commission even recommended grants to them as a proper charge on public funds.'[29] As grant-in-aid system was recommended by the Hunter Commission for making progress in the field of education.

Challenges in the Field of Missionaries

Undoubtedly, from the above description it's clear that missionaries are the real heroes who took up the cause of the progress of women education not only in United Provinces, but in all over the India. The plight of the women became one of the major issues not only for the Indian social reformers but also for the Missionaries. However, this job was not the easy one, as women were deeply in the chain of social prejudices and social customs which was deeply rooted in the Hindu religious arena. To get rid from this chain, was the one main task for the social reformers and for the missionaries also, who really wanted to see a free and an independent woman in India, in fact in every corner of the India.

The different customs like Sati, child marriage, female infanticide, purdah system etc., prevailed not only up to the British period rather than continued to be frequently practiced in the province, during the colonial period. To raise the inferior status of Indian woman in the society was the main challenge in front of the missionaries. They felt that a good deal of work is needed to change this attitude towards the advancement of the education of women.[30]

At the time of annexation of Oudh, and from that till the British ruled the India, women were facing many kinds of problems in terms of their education, as education for them was considered unnecessary, unorthodox and also seems to be very dangerous if they study. The different social norms were one of the major obstacles in the way of women education of Oudh or in United Provinces. As the Orthodox life of the society of the provinces and different social evils of the society are keeping women away from education.

Different Measures Took up by the Native People of U.P. for the Progress of Missionaries Education

Extension of missionary education as towards at the end of the 19th century was not only processed by Europeans and missionaries, rather than Indian society played a crucial role in expanding the educational enterprises. Indian demand mostly for mission schools for instruction was absolute necessary thing. Basically mission schools and their educational activities rely on most of elite Indian people as from urban and rural both. Mission education proved to be popular among Indian societies as it saw the form of welfare of the Indian people. Missions had this (education) as a useful tool for the social transformation.

There were countless and numerous examples to show that how Indian princess and high officials were interested in to the promotion of missionary enterprise. Like in Benaras, the LMS College was financially supported with an annual grant of Rs 120 by the Maharaja of the city.'[31] Another Raja from Agra namely, Chaudhari Amar Singh, provided CMS with thirteen acres of land mainly for the site of a Christian hotel. These Rajas also demanded to have possibly more female teachers at their opened schools. They also tried to have equal literacy among Hindus husband and wives. Many influential Zamindars maintained to spend their money in constructing mission schools in United Provinces. As one of the efficient Brahman doctor asked the CMS to also open one of the girls schools and also asked to contribute towards this step.'[32]

As far as Agra was concerned, where a group of Kayasthas[33] mainly took the initiative to run and manage their own schools, later on some of which came under mission management by somehow at the request of the Kayasthas sabhas. With the passage of time, local government and municipalities, themselves funded and encouraged the growth of many mission schools. They also showed their interests in their promotion. One of the Indian member belongs to the municipal council in Meerut, positively supported an increased grant to the CMS high school for their native people. Similarly, one of the CMS orphanages in Gorakhpur was later on turned in to a girls Anglo-Vernacular school due to the pressure as well as demand at the local level.[34] All these examples shows that there is a growing demand of mission education in United Provinces not only from pundits, Rajas and different high Zamindars, but majority were also from middle and less elite people at local rural communities. They were highly influenced by their efforts and dedication towards the education of boys and girls.

Lack of Trained Teachers and Lady Inspectresses

Appointment of trained teachers especially female in both government and in aided schools and colleges were the major hurdle in obtaining education to women, as there is a lack of trained staff. Efforts to extend education among the women in U.P. seemed to be useless if there will be no female staff. In most of the schools even in girls schools there were majority of male teachers and staff, which resulted in less admission of girls in to the schools. Mostly public schools suffered from this. As most of the aided school were having ladies connected with the missionary societies. Mr. White mentioned in his report that in Lucknow district, most of the schools have the advantages of superintendence by a special inspectresses in which greater success is recorded.[35] There is still want of well behaved and efficient mistresses in the provinces. The appointment of male teachers mainly lost the confidence of the parents. Mostly parents became insecure to send their girls or daughters in those schools. With the coming of the years, there is a growing demand of trained teachers and also lady inspectress to look after the girls school, and also to have a look on their progress. This seems to be great and major obstacles in the progress of female education in U.P. Although, very few Indian girls forward their education even beyond an elementary stage, when female teachers can be drawn in a very limited numbers. They are hardly to found. 'In the case of United Provinces, female teachers are very rare. This difficulty hinder the growth of female education in the provinces. There is a non-supply of female teachers. Prejudice mostly came in this way. One of the normal schools of Lucknow for female teachers has at last been established, and it also hoped that the different arrangements would be able to meet the requirements of the purdah system will commend themselves to the native people.[36] Many training institutes were opened to improve the supply of teachers. Nevertheless, the missionaries also contributed by providing trained female teachers to the govt. schools as to promote female education.

Text Books and Curriculum for Girls School

The missionaries also put their focus to improve or to maintain the appropriate curriculum of the girl's school. They made certain kind of changes according to the needs of the quality of education. Proper curriculum was the basic need for the govt. and missions in their schools. Apart from the domestic knowledge they should possess knowledge about the drawing, needle work, arithmetic, geography, history etc. There is a desire to make efforts in the changes in the curriculum of their girl's school as to get match for their social needs also. English was the only subject that was much debated. 'English was prohibited in the preparatory and lower primary classes would presumably be equally applicable to the case of girls, but the managers of girl's school which was maintained by the missionaries bodies have not observed the orders and are reluctant to do so. Actually, they don't agree that it is undesirable to teach English pari passu with a vernacular to beginners, and they allege that Christian parents at any rate prefer that their girls should learn English from the very beginning.'3[7] So, missionaries focused more on the English subject as to introduce in almost most of the mission schools. They want that girls should learn English languages apart from their vernacular languages. Curriculum and text-books mainly differs for girls and boys at different stages. Mostly girls were omitted away from the manual training, agriculture and all. But needle-work and drawing seems to be continued and also some attempt was made to introduce domestic economy and hygiene like subjects, so that girls could have knowledge about this.

During 1915, there is an appointment of committee mainly to discuss about the curriculum for Anglo-vernacular and vernacular schools for girls.[38]

Subjects of Study in Preparatory Section

A. (1) Reading (Urdu/Hindi)

(2) Writing (ditto)

(3) Arithmetic

(4) Sewing

(5) Drawing on black board (optional)

(6) Brush-Work (do)

(7) Clay-modeling (do)

(8) Kindergarten games (do)

B. (1) Reading (Urdu/ Hindi)

(2) Writing (ditto)

(3) Arithmetic

(4) Sewing

(5) Drawing on black board (optional)

(6) Brush-Work

(7) Clay-modeling

(8) Kindergarten games

In Lower Primary Section

Class I

(1) Reading (Urdu/Hindi)

(2) Writing (ditto)

(3) Arithmetic

(4) Sewing

(5) Drawing on black board (optional)

(6) Brush-Work

(7) Geography

(8) Object Lesson

(9) Clay Modeling

(10) Calisthenics

Class II

(1) Reading (Urdu/ Hindi)

(2) Writing (ditto)

(3) Arithmetic

(4) Sewing

(5) Simple practical direction in hygiene

(6) Drawing

(7) Brush-Work

(8) Geography

(9) Object Lessons

(10) Clay Modeling

(11) Calisthenics (optional)

In Upper Primary Section

Class III

(1) English

(2) Vernacular (Urdu/Hindi)

(3) Arithmetic

(4) Geography

(5) Sewing

(6) Simple practice direction in hygiene.

(7) Drawing (optional)

(8) Brush-Work

(9) Object Lessons

(10) Clay Modeling

(11) Calisthenics

(12) Cooking

Class IV

(1) English

(2) Vernacular (Urdu/Hindi)

(3) Arithmetic

(4) Geography

(5) Sewing

(6) Informal Instruction in hygiene.

(7) Drawing (optional)

(8) Brush-Work

(9) Object Lessons

(10) Clay Modeling

(11) Calisthenics

(12) Cooking

In Lower Middle Section

Class V and VI

(1) English

(2) Vernacular (Urdu/Hindi)

(3) Arithmetic

(4) Geography

(5) Domestic Science with Sewing

(6) Two or three of the following alternative subjects----

(a) History stories

(b) Drawing

(c) Brush-work

(d) A classical language (Persian, Arabic, or Sanskrit)

(7) Nature Study

(8) Cooking (optional)

Upper Middle Section

Class VII and VIII

(1) Arithmetic

(2) History and Geography

(3) Domestic science

(4) Two or three of the following alternative subjects

(a) English

(b) Vernacular (Urdu/Hindi)

(c) A classical language (Urdu/Hindi)

(d) Drawing

(e) Algebra and geometry

(5) Cooking (optional)

High Section

Classes IX and X

(1) Arithmetic

(2) History and Geography

(3) Domestic science

(4) Sewing

(5) Two or three of the following alternative subjects

(a) English

(b) Vernacular (Urdu/Hindi)

(c) A classical language (Urdu/Hindi)

(d) Drawing

(e) Algebra and geometry

(6) Cooking (optional)

So, from the above mentioned curriculum schools for Anglo-vernacular and from vernacular schools for girls, these subjects were mentioned in their schools. All these descriptions shows that there was the all basic subjects in your classes according to the need.

System of Grant-in-Aid and Expenditure

Different schools like govt. schools and aided, and another types of schools had avail the system of grant. Mostly more grants were given to the girls schools as compared to boy's schools, so as to promote female education in the provinces. Different types of grants like grant for different equipments, grant for buildings etc. are made in to the provisions of the Indian education Commission of 1882. Earlier less grant was made to the govt. schools but later on with the passage of time more grant was given to the girls schools as compared to boys school. IIC of 1882 suggested, that grants-in-aid were given with undiscriminating liberality to all promoters of girls schools.[39] Later on it also suggests that, between 1871 and 1881 a great decrease took place in girls schools.

There abolition was mainly due to the financial position of the govt. in 1876, as later on more grants-in-aid have recently been assigned to schools unaided.[40] United Province mainly lacked in the matter of women education, as because of the one reason that less grant was supported to the girls of the provinces as compared to the other provinces.Sometime girls were allowed to read in boys school also. Girls schools want more security as compared to boys schools. It costs more than boys schools. There is a need of larger extension of female education. Girls schools desires to have more female teachers, female inspectors, female surveillance on the way to and from school, sometime needed to have hotel arrangement for girl only who came from distant area. That's why it costs more than boys school.

Mission schools seemed to have more funds. Some help they got from govt. side, and majority of help and fund they got from different mission societies and later on from the elite persons of the United Provinces who were really impressed by their way of instruction towards female education. The table given below shows the expenditure made on secondary and primary schools for girls during the year of 1885-1886.

Table 4.7

Expenditure on Secondary and Primary schools for Girls in 1885-86

	From Provincial Revenues		
Provinces	**In Schools under Public management**	**In Aided schools**	**From Municipal and local funds**
	Rs	Rs	Rs
Madras	47015	121202	11401
Bombay	31652	40573	54941
Bengal	17205	127488	7264
N.W.P	-	38101	46218
Punjab	9351	52103	20632
C.P	7176	10601	8443
Assam	2995	775	7111
Berar	996	-	5155
Coorg	-	264	110
Burma	-	18132	20185
Total	116350	409239	181460
Total for 1884-85	105779	368792	174648

Source: S. Bhattacharya, The Development of Women's Education In India: A Collection of Documents 1850-1920, p.166.

From the above table it is clear that there is different expenditure from different types of sources in different provinces. Over all, there is an increase towards this field from different sources, but according to this table under public management school no expenditure was made during this particular year, as compared to aided schools in NWP, more efforts were made. In different provinces there is more expenditure as compared to NWP. It's clear that girls schools are more supported by private management in every provinces of India, i.e. there is more progress of girls education in other provinces. Similarly in the year of 1913, the amount allotted to United Provinces on Education bore this as well.[41]

Category	**Allocation (in Rupees)**
Primary education	303000
Girls education	70000
Secondary education	95000

Above data reveals that very less amount was expended on girls education as well as on India had given grant of Rs. 7 lakhs mainly for primary education during the year of 1912-1913; one of the main reason of less progress in attendance at schools was due to shortness of money.[42] Not much of money was expended on girls education from the side of govt. In 1908, recurring grant of six lakhs for primary education was released and in that six lakhs rupees, only one lakh was total estimated for female education.[43]

With the passage of time more aided schools were seems to be opened for girls. Actually, the thing is that the growth of education mainly in the second half of the 19th century was partnership between the state and the private management. To add more resource in the education system private enterprise allowed to enter by the British government. The result was that the system of grant-in-aid was mainly started to seek more help from private cooperation. The earlier schools for girls was low in the provinces, and simultaneously due to the financial crisis, the British govt. found themselves less efficient in promoting female education. So, more private enterprise (mission society) took the further expansion of female schools in Oudh (U.P.) and many other provinces of India. Mainly grant-in-aid system was introduced as to bring private enterprise under state control, mostly to improve the quality of instruction among different schools and almost to create uniformity in the whole process of education. Different types of grant was made to the different types of aided schools. Public opinion, also too favoured an increase in state share in private schools. Grants were also made to Zenana mission schools also. Apart from this different Anglo-vernacular girls schools were also maintained by the funds from Christian missions. And this mainly comes from private funds coming from local and foreign sources. In the coming years the funds was raised to meet out the different expenses related to girls education. J.S Cotton reveals in his report on education in India for 1892-97, 'that total expenditure has risen but most of the from private funds. Less effort was made from govt. side. Crosthwaite Girls school situated at Lucknow, which is mainly an unaided Anglo-vernacular school for the higher education of native ladies of Lucknow enjoys the endowment of about two lakhs of rupees mainly from private enterprise. Anglo-vernacular schools doing great work as reported by Miss D' Abreu.'[44] There is a desire of more grant for girls education. Different sources revealed that aided schools revealed more money for girls education. Missionaries also funding to the aided higher school. Like IT college at Lucknow, occupies an important place in the educational field. The income of the college consists of[45]:

1. Mission grant–14000 Rs
2. Mission grant pay of 5 missionaries including–12350 Rs
   Furlough allowances
3. Fees–6200 Rs
4. Govt. grants–6731 Rs
   Total = 39281

The figures above show that more fund was from mission. Also, different foreign missionary society funded this college. The result was that different scholars from different other provinces attended this college. This college also has good buildings which attract girls from all over provinces. As mostly girls schools and colleges had not proper buildings, staff and equipments, which found one of the obstacles in girls education. Most of the missions schools and college received more grant every year.

Students Hostels by Missionaries

One of the major factors which were taken up by the missionaries was the student hostel. The student hostel undoubtedly offered very personal kind of attraction and interaction which mainly started by the missionaries. Numerous hostels were opened in different districts of U.P. like in Allahabad, Kanpur, Benaras and in Lucknow also, with major proportions of scholars in hostel, which was mainly supplied by the govt. As many of the govt. hostels were poor in condition, this was really an important opportunity which missionaries saw to expand their enterprise, as well as to increase their influence.

There was the demand of residential system among boys and girls. The demand was shaped by an acute system of Indian education for mainly English and Anglo-vernacular education. In the different districts like in Allahabad, Kanpur, Benaras, Lucknow, mission schools understood the requirements of hostel by the many student, this was seen as an opportunity to acquire the attention of the students. In total expansion of missionaries hostel up to and after 1900 was totally significant in their respect.[46]

Table 4.8

Growth of mission hostels in the United Provinces, 1903-1908

	1903	**1908**
Boys hostel	270	401
No. of Boarders	6875	12577
Girls hostel	32	43
No. of Boarders	2311	3228

Source: Hayden, J.A. Bellenoit, Missionary Education and Empire in Late Colonial India, 1860-1920, p.156

Above mentioned table clearly gives the rising demand and expansion of hostel among boys and girls of United Provinces. This growth was explosive and significant in united Provinces. The CMS also ran majority of hostel in the United Provinces.[47] By the year of 1911, they were successful in opening the numerous hostel in Agra, Allahabad, Benaras, Sikanderabad. Similarly another one, SPG, also released the grant of Rs 3000 for the construction of hostel for both Hindus and Muslim students in Kanpur college.[48]

Apart from all this, missions were also successful in opening of the hostel in respect of women also. There was also the demand of women's hostels among the scholars. Nevertheless, the educational enterprise were managed to get some 4000 female scholars in their hostel.[49] Basically, most of the efforts were in promoting Zenana education, because most of the Indian men do not allow their girl child to stay in a hostel. But, in contrast missionaries were involved in educating Indian women, and also providing them the accommodation also. For example, the Oxford and Cambridge hostel in Allahabad, was mostly funded by the amount of missions.[50] In the hostel which was mostly funded by missionaries, students of any caste could reside here. This was mainly aimed at bridging the gap between the students of different caste or religion. In this way they could have a interactive culture. Maintaining hostel was an perfect example to fulfill the feeling of brotherhood among the scholars of different background. For example, the St. Stephen's, St. John's along with the Oxford and Cambridge hostel of Allahabad were all relatively prominently institutions among all. Allahabad was one of the educational centres of education. Their building of hostel was one of the finest among all, and also well connected in the educational enterprise. All this shows the dedication and the efforts of missionaries in the promotion of education among the people of United Provinces.

From the above description we will get the gloomy picture of female education led by the missionaries in United Provinces. No doubt, they are the pioneers in promoting the female education in the provinces by various efforts, also from the help of various missionaries agencies who played a crucial role in promoting female education. Missionaries' educational enterprise was totally inseparable in the field of education.

FOOTNOTES

1. Suresh Chandra Ghosh, The History of Education in Modern India 1757-2012, p.9.
2. Ibid., p.11
3. Y.B. Mathur, *Women's Education in India 1813-1966.*, p.4
4. J.P.Naik and Syed Nurullah, A History of Education in India, MacMillan, p.115.
5. Ibid., p.115
6. Y.B. Mathur, *Women's Education in India 1813-1966*, p.21.

7. Hayden Bellenoit, Education, Missionaries and the Indian Nation, c.1880-1920, ed. Parimala V. Rao., p.177.
8. The first missionary appointed by the Baptist Society in India.
9. Sabyasachi Bhattacharya, *The Development of Women's Education in India; A Collection of Documents* 1850-1920., p.49.
10. Ibid., p.49.
11. Ibid., p.49.
12. Sabyasachi Bhattacharya, *The Development of Women's Education in India: A Collection of Documents* 1850-1920., p.61.
13. Ibid., 171.
14. Administrative report of NWP and Oudh 1887-1888, Allahabad.
15. Sabyasachi Bhattacharya, *The Development of Women's Education in India: A Collection of Documents* 1850-1920., pp. 282-284.
16. Ibid., p.300.
17. Ibid., p.326
18. Ibid., p.327.
19. Minna G. Cowan, *The Education of the Women of India-Primary Source Edition*, p. 45.
20. Administrative Report of NWP and Oudh 1899-1900, for the year, ending 31st March 1900, Allahabad, Printed at NWP and Oudh Govt. Press, 1901.
21. Administrative Report of United Provinces of Agra and Oudh, 1902-1903.
22. Ibid.
23. Administrative Report of United Provinces of Agra and Oudh, 1911- 1912.
24. Administrative Report of United Provinces of Agra and Oudh, 1925-1926, Lucknow, 1927.
25. File no. 56/1921, Isabella Thoburn College, Lucknow.
26. Ibid.
27. Minna G. Cowan, *The Education of the Women of India-Primary Source Edition*, Fleming H Rewell Company, New York, 1912.
28. William Hunter, Report of the Indian Education Commission, 1882-83, p. 535.
29. Ibid.
30. Y.B. Mathur, Women's Education in India 1813-1966, Asia Publishing House, Bombay, 1973., p.21.

31. Hayden. J.A. Bellenoit, *Missionary Education and Empire in Late Colonial India*, 1860-1920, Pickering and Chatto London, 2007., p. 113.
32. Ibid., p.114
33. A Hindu Caste
34. Hayden. J.A. Bellenoit, *Missionary Education and Empire in Late Colonial India*, 1860-1920, Pickering and Chatto London, 2007., p. 115.
35. S. Bhattacharya, *The Development of Women's Education in India: A Collection of Documents 1850-1920*., p. 172
36. Ibid., p.348.
37. File no. 95 of 1912, Proposal to prohibit the teaching of English below class iii in recognised Anglo- Vernacular Schools for girls, Education Deptt.
38. File no. 252 of 1915, Appointment of a Committee to consider the curriculum for Anglo- Vernacular Schools for girls, 1918, Govt. of United Provinces, August, Proceeding no. 15 and 16, Education Deptt.
39. File no. 3 of 1884, Report of the Indian Education Commission, Education Deptt.
40. Ibid.
41. File no. 229 of 1912, Three years programme of requirements for Female Education, Govt. of United Provinces, June Proceeding no. 31 and 32, Edu. Deptt.
42. File no. 38 of 1912, Imperial grant for the extension and Improvement of Primary Education in the United Provinces, May Proceeding no. 70 to 74, Educ. Deptt.
43. File no. 120 of 1908, Recurring Grant of six lakhs for Primary Education, Proceeding no. 11 and 12, Govt. of U.P., Educ. Deptt..
44. S. Bhattacharya, The Development of Women's Education in India: A Collection of Documents 1850-1920., pp. 283-284.
45. File no. 56 of 1921, Isabella Thobourn College Lucknow.
46. Hayden J.A. Bellenoit, Missionary Education and Empire in Late Colonial India, 1860-1920., p. 156.
47. Hayden J.A. Bellenoit, Missionary Education and Empire in Late Colonial India, 1860-1920., p156.
48. Ibid., pp. 156-157.
49. Ibid., p.157.
50. Ibid., p.158.

6

Social Reformers and Development of Women Education

There is no doubt that status of women education was quite deplorabale as compared to men in United Provinces or in any other provinces of India. Basically education as an opportunity was always remained untouched in the case of women. They could not use it fully as in early decades. Educational opportunities for girls were very rare as different cruel socials were going on not only in United Provinces but in all over the India. Basically, to get rid from all these cruel evils from 18th century till the first half of the 20th century, different social reformers both male and female took the cause of different issues related to women, and also maintained their dignity in the society with lot of efforts, and also uplifted their social, educational and political status in the society. The main motto of social reformers was to create equality between men and women. They want a society which was free from all types of discrimination and differences, which continued throughout in the society. They want to create a new definition of women and their new image. They want that they should realize their own rights. Women should not depend on others for anything. Moreover, the attempts at reform were chiefly motivated by an ideological acceptance of the liberal rationalist values typical of the west. As some of the reformers believes that the Indian education was not up to the mark and was not appropriate to grow the personality of an individual or women. Traditional type of education was followed in Indian society, rather than there should be some western ideas, that should bring some changes in the social customs. From the 19th century, different types of social reform movement took place by several different social reformers as to make some contribution to the progress made by Indian women in many fields.

Basically, the nineteenth century is known as the century of different kinds of social reforms in India that gave birth to a kind of 'renaissance'. It started from Bengal and later on spread to various parts of India. Majority of the social reformers are from the presidencies provinces. But, with the efforts of these reformers tremendous changes were brought in the position and status of Indian women by giving them education and also by passing different social legislations. During the colonial rule, some European writers divided the historical account of Indian women as 'Orientalists' and 'Utilitarious'. The first group of writers i.e., the Orientalists believed that there was a 'golden era' in the Vedic times which was totally free from all types of discrimination as well as we have great learned women scholars, which shows that women were too acquainted higher education as compared to men. On the other hand, Utilitarians, believed that the Indian society was full of corrupt practices, and there was no golden age era, moreover the condition and status of women was inferior from the very beginning. From this type of discussion as a criticism to the Indian social system especially by the Utilitarian gave birth to a new group of writers called as a nationalists who strongly oppose the ideas of Utilitarian and believed that 'golden era' existed as the Vedic period, where women enjoyed a higher status in the society, at once in the society. In Hindu society the position of women during the period i.e. from 1850 up to 1950, was undoubtedly low, inferior as well as subordinate by men.

The advent of the British in India had brought not only a new form of government, but also a new kind of knowledge, new ideas, new innovation and new technology. Earlier the British education system also did not benefitted Indian women as it limited only up to the higher class of society. It was the only social reformers from all over the country who had shown their deep concern over the different issues like sati, child marriage, female infanticide, widowhood, purdah, polygamy, devdasi and most important subject i.e. the 'denial of education' to them. As women were less educated as compared to men, because of it a nation can't grow on social level, economic level, political level and on educational level.

This chapter has been divided in to 2 phases. In first phase shall discuss the well known reformers on global level like Raja Ram Mohan Roy, Annie Beasant, Gopal Krishna Gokhale, Lala Lajpat Rai, Pandit Madan Mohan Malviya, Pandita Ramabai, Sarojini Naidu, Mahadevi Verma etc. who worked for the up-liftment of women on different issues like education and strictly prohibited the different types of evils that lower the status of women in the society, and also try to throw light on the views about the promotion of education or women education. On the other hand, next phase will discuss about the some eminent official intellectual persons especially from the United Provinces who took up the cause to promote women education by their different kinds of speeches or by some kinds of resolutions. These persons are not very famous on global level but without them the discussion about women emancipation or upliftment in the United Provinces was incomplete. So, lets discuss about some of the major social reformers on global level, as the list is endless, but then also some of the social reformers hold an important place when there is a discussion about women welfare.

Raja Ram Mohan Roy (1772-1833)

First and foremost reformer of India who eminently worked for the upliftment of the women in the society was Raja Ram Mohan Roy (1772-1833). This name is usually listed first among the reformers of 19th century as improving women's status in the society. He had been called by the different names like "father of modern India", "champion of women's rights", "father of renaissance", and some a "feminist" also. Somewhere Raja Ram Mohan Roy personally experienced the lower condition of women in his life, that's why he took extreme effort by bringing up their status. Raja Ram Mohan Roy was a versatile man with eminent personality. As he know different types of languages and meanwhile he was influenced by the culture of the west. 'In 1815 he started Atmiya Sabha (spiritual association). He carried a struggle against the religious and social evils.[1] He wanted to spread scientific, literacy and political knowledge among the Indian people. 'In 1829, Raja Ram Mohan Roy founded Brahma Sabha' to purify Hinduism from the evils of orthodoxy, superstition and ritualism.[2] Later on it became Brahmo Samaj. Apart from the different objectives of Brahmo Samaj, it highly emphasized on "equality". It believes that all men and women are equal. The Brahmo Samaj opposed different evils like polygamy, child marriage and Sati system and last but not least the untouchability. These are the different evils which were prevailing in the society during that time. Because of this women were suppressed in the society and not allowed to get education. Raja Ram Mohan Roy was famous for his long and successful campaign for the abolition of 'Sati', as self immolation of widows on the funeral pyre of their husbands. He wrote many articles on this matter. The custom of Sati was the most furious social evil in the eighteenth and early nineteenth century. The practice of Sati was prevalent in the Hindu society from a very long period of time.

Raja Ram Mohan Roy published many books in Bengali and majority of them reinsulated in to English for defense of practice of Sati. 'In 1818 his first tract was published and in 1819 the second one in Bengali and also translated it in 1820. He said in his works that, Manu was the greatest, the most famous and trustworthy law giver might alone would be equal to any doze others put together. Later on he cited–let her emaciate her body by living voluntarily on pure flowers, roots and fruits, but let her not, when her Lord is deceased, even pronounce the name of another man, let her continue till death forgiving all injuries, performing harsh duties, avoiding every seasonal pleasure and cheerful practicing the incomparable rules of virtue which have been followed by such woman as were devoted to only one husband.[3] Later on his second tract in 1819, he said, the practice, therefore, of forcibly trying down woman to the pile and burning them to death is inconsistent with the shastras and highly sinful. It is of no consequence to affirm that this customary in any particular country if it were universally practiced the murders would still be criminal. The pretence, that may be followed in matters where no particular rules are prescribed in the shastra, is not to be justified by the practice of few.[4] His draft shows that he did not want that sati would no longer should be practiced in any parts of India.

In 1818, he also submitted a petition to the governor-general. He also appealed that punish the murders of sati who compel the widows to burn themselves. Rather than to help her for her future, or to encourage her to pursue higher education in life, this cruel society and poor mindset of people especially male counterparts forcefully encourage them to be Sati. Ultimately, Lord William Bentick the governor-general declared 'Sati' as illegal and punishable by the court on 4th December 1829. Raja Ram Mohan Roy always encourage women for their betterment. He also emphasized more on women's education and worked for their progress. Somehow it felt that as to somewhere to get rid from the different cruel evils Raja Ram Mohan Roy supported modern education in India, as modern education was looked upon by him as a major instrument to bring radical change in the society as well as in the status of women. Roy had tremendous capacity of organizing his thoughts and put them in to the practice. His Brahmo Samaj did a lot to improve the social status of women. Because improvement in the social status is must as after getting rid from the different evils, women can pot focus on their education or how to progress in life. These hilarious evils were really responsible for the degraded status of women society. In this case, he was not only a herald of new age but one of the architects of modern India. Sarojini Naidu aptly described Ram Mohan as "the reconciler of irreconcilables".

Annie Beasant

Next reformer, which comes to our mind who rigorously worked for women welfare was none other than Annie Beasant. She was a Victorian radical whose outspoken views included advocacy of women's rights and opposition to British imperial policies. Meanwhile she came to India. She has done resisting efforts to reform the status of Indian women.[5] In 1874 by delivering a lecture on 'the political status of women' she had shown her keen interest in the emancipation of women welfare. Annie Beasant was an Irish lady, she was so much concerned about the upliftment of Indian women, and that's why in 1893 she invented a "Theosophical society". Annie Beasant had interested herself in the education of Indian women and had attempted to make them conscious of their social and political rights, so that they could raise themselves in future and be educated. During 1890's, she defended the different Hindu social customs and also countered the efforts of Indian social reformers, who had been working to improve the social status of women.

Annie Beasant's dedication towards the education of Indian girls or women was truly shown in 1898 where she established Central Hindu College in Benaras, by giving training to boys in their Hindu heritage along with the fusion of western scientific knowledge. Later on she opened another school for girls at Benaras namely Girl's school (Besant Kanya Mahavidyalaya). She opened this school as she firmly believed that women's emancipation could be achieved only after the removal of illiteracy among the women, and for this there should be a direct connection between women's education and national reconstruction. As to inculcate a spirit of patriotism among girls, the emphasis should be made more on the teaching of Sanskrit and Vernacular literature. At the same hand she too offered to support girls education by giving some recommendation as how to improve girls education in India. 'During her visit to Maharani's Girl's school in Mysore in 1896, she advocated girls as "your elder sister, with a white face but a Hindu heart", education was important, but they should always remember that "purity is more than learning and a noble character is greater than success in books.....Worship the God, Obey your parents and husband, and be like flowers, whose sweet fragrance perfumes all the houses.'[6] Beasant focused more on the improvement of female education. Meanwhile she also focused on the curriculum of girls and gives her recommendations to improve the curriculum of girls, because she believed that by introducing right kind of curriculum and syllabus for girls in school is the only way to improve the status of women education. Beasant's pronouncements on reform and her work for female education brought praise from the Indian National Reformers which enlightened them also to work more against women education, and they viewed like Mrs. Beasant is slowly coming round. The fit of spirituality is passing away, and she is opening her eyes to the hard facts which surround mankind in their mundane experience .... Mrs. Beasant has become wise, and we hope, as she learns more of the country, she will become wiser still.[7]

Later on in one pamphlet during 1904, she briefly described on the type of education for Indian girls. Annie Beasant put all the essential and desirable things of education for Indian girls. First thing she focused as the fundamental doctrines of every religion should be taught in clear, simple and in rational method. Some kind of Sanskrit, Persian or Arabic or classical language according to the girls religion must be taught to them. Later on she focused on the study of history and geography should be taught to them. 'The hygiene of the household should be thoroughly taught. Apart from this some knowledge of simple medicines is needed by every mother so that she may not be instantly calling a doctor, she should be able to deal with the accidental injuries. Sufficient arithmetic is also very essential to learn as to keep an account of all household purposes. A knowledge of cookery has also been part of the education of the Indian housewife, and this should still have its place in education, or there will be little comfort in the house for husband and children. Drawing and painting should also be focused with some artistic embroidery and needle work of all kinds. In short they should learn all kind of sewing, darning and the cutting out of such made garments as are used in their districts.'[8] All these outlines made by her about education seems to be adequate according to the needs of the young daughters of India and also bring them in to useful and cultured women as heads of happy households, "lights of the home".

Later on in 1915, again she focused on women education as published in her commonweal in April 16, 1915. She explains that in India, now a great wave of change is passing over Indian womanhood. Anyone who has visited various parts of the country they could see a new aspirations stirring in the hearts of Indian women at the present time. By the different kinds of the speeches through by different woman speaker made a deep mark on the heart, mind and soul of the Indian woman. 'Those who judge of the educational status of Indian women by the census test of literacy go very far astray in their opinions.[9]

At last, she believed that Indian greatness will not be able to restore until the Indian womanhood could be able to obtain a larger, a freer and a fuller life. The power of woman to uplift or debase man is practically unlimited, and man and woman must walk forward as in hand-in-hand to the raising of India, otherwise she will never be raised at all. Views of Annie Beasant was quietly very impressive about the education of Indian girls and meanwhile shows her efforts, care about Indian women.

Gopal Krishna Gokhale

Gopal Krishna Gokhale, was one of the supporters of female education. Gokhale was known by his Compulsory Education Bill of 1910, as this Bill put emphasis on the compulsory education of boys as he did not propose it as compulsion for the present for girls. He is of the view that 'for girls for the present and for some years to come, education will have to be on a voluntary basis. In the context of girl's, education was more important than of boys in the India of today.'[10] His views somewhere reflects his interest in women education. A wide diffusion of female education in all its branches is a factor of the highest value to the true well-being of every nation. He believes that there is bound of caste and customs which lower the education of women in India. They are the victims of customs, are hurtful in the highest degree. The main thing is to emancipate their minds. He is of the view that in ancient times they had very honored position. 'In our great epic poems-descriptive of a period subsequent to the Upanishads, but still considerably anterior to the Christian era–they are represented as going through a regular course of education, of which drawing, music and even dancing (which is now considered degrading) formed part; even they mixed freely with men and entered in to learned discussions on spiritual or any other difficult subjects. They fully participate in debates. Later on in late 11th century as with the advent of Muslim invaders we can find instances of women having high degree of education and also engaged in intellectual pursuits. Then, almost suddenly, all light seemed to be extinguished, and for the last seven centuries our female world has been enveloped in a kind of intellectual gloom....'[11] "These views of Gokhale about women education seems that according to him women growing herself by centuries and centuries and a new kind of intellectual gloom could be seen among them.

Lala Lajpat Rai

Lala Lajpat Rai was one of the most Extremist leader. He was also in favor of women education. He saw boy and girl on the same footing as equal to each other. He did not felt any kind of discrimination among both of them. He believed that the main aim of education is to make fit both men and women for the battle of life. They should not be converted in to anchorites and ascetics. They are the new citizens of tomorrow. They should take the best advantage from life as from them some our next statesmen, administrators, generals, inventors, captains of industry, manufacturers as well as more philosophers, thinkers and teachers. Later he emphasized more on that 'we are beginning to realize that the best social thinkers of the world have been those who were brought up in the full blaze of the social conditions of the time and who had personal experience of how men in general lived, and how they acted and reacted on each other.'[12] Although he believed that boys and girls should move equally in life and both of them should take equal opportunities in life as to move further. He is of the view that boys should not be brought up in isolation, and girls should not properly be brought up in Purdah, as it make both of them a very poor man and woman. Later on he says that, 'often they have been succumbing to the first temptation they came across. They wreck their lives from want of experience and want of nerve. I am speaking from actual experience. Not that men educated in ordinary schools and colleges are always better, but that at least the former have not shown any superiority in handling situations which arise from being thrown in to social conditions to which they were strangers before.[13] Lala Lajpat Rai's views on women education shows that he is very frank person with frank ideas. He believes that by bringing them together truly a nation can develop and we can have well equipped and educated society. Both of them should be treated more as comrades, instead of dependents on anybody or inferior and subordinates. We should try to fill in them the fullest confidence as to fight for any kind of social battle in life. Try to encourage with absolute frankness in them. Instead of keeping in them distance or any kind of discrimination, try to bring them on equal footing of life. Any kind of prejudice and sentiment should not come in their progress.

Pandita Ramabai

Another name which comes in to our mind that is none other than Pandita Ramabai. Pandita Ramabai (1858-1922) was born in to a Chitpavan Brahman family. Her father was held high esteem in

Sanskrit, and she received her training in Sanskrit from her parents. Later she studied Vedas and Shastras, and came to called as 'Pandita' for her Sanskrit scholarship. As she travelled in various parts of India, and saw the very deplorable conditions of Hindu women in the different provinces like Madras, Bombay, Punjab, North-West provinces and many more. These things lead her to work for the progress of women. She came in to contact with some social reformers, when she went to Pune. After coming in to contact with these reformers she was infused with the kind of spirit as to make some substantial contributions to make a better women, particularly in the field of education. As later on she established Arya Mahila Samaj as spread branches all over in Maharashtra.

Pandit Ramabai's work, The high caste Hindu women, was published in 1888 in Philadelphia. This work mainly meant for foreign readers who had a curiosity to know about social customs of the Hindus. This work by her mainly gives the description about the condition of women in India by analyzing their childhood, married life and widowhood and also throw light that how they were marginalized by men. Later on she also established 'Sharda Sadan' in Mumbai. The main motto behind this institution was to provide an asylum to the destitute high caste widows. As a result of this many high caste girls and young widows enrolled themselves in the Sadan to attain education. Ramabai firmly believes that the caste system was one of the negative aspects of the Hindu society. She believes that caste affiliations, encouraged narrow self-interest and was a big (impediment) hindrance in the development of democratic and social values. This seems to be main reason why she encouraged the women of her Sadan to adopt Christianity, though not by forcefully, but by choice. Undoubtedly, contributions made by her really progressed by all women of different caste and appreciated by different reformers and also by her contemporaries.

Sarojini Naidu

Sarojini Naidu was born in Hyderabad of a Bengali Brahmin family, on 13th February, 1879. Her father, Dr. Aghorenath Chattopadhyaya was an educationist and a leading scientist. Naidu was a staunch supporter of women education, being a nationalist she became the supporter of women's right at very early age. Apart from the supporter in the education for women, she also created awareness among the women for their political right and for this she organized and lead a powerful agitation in England on behalf of the women of India. Speaking to the Indian social conference at Calcutta by addressing the views regarding the education of Indian women:

'It is still necessary for us to stand upon public platforms and should pass resolution in favour of what is called female education in India. She believes that, there is not even an unanimous acceptance of the fact that the education of women is an essential factor in the process of nation-building. The word education is the most misunderstood word in any language........ The instruction being merely the accumulation of knowledge might, indeed, lend itself to conventional definition, but education is an immeasurable, beautiful, indispensable atmosphere in which we like and move and have one being. Does one man dare to deprive another of his birthright to God's pure air which nourishes his body ?... How then small a man dare to deprive a human soul of its immemorial inheritance of liberty and life? Your fathers, in depriving your mothers of that immemorial birthright have robbed you, their sons, of your just inheritance. Therefore, I charge you, restore your women their ancient rights, far, as I have said, it is we, and not you, who are the real nation-builders, and without our active co-operation at all points of progress all our Congresses and Conferences are in vain. Educate your women and the nation will take care of itself, for it is as true today as it was yesterday and will be to the end of human life that the hand that rocks the cradle rules the world.'[14]

All her views create a kind of consciousness among women, as she was trying to create a new kind of awareness among the women. Later on, she says that, women are suffering from centuries to centuries instead of knowing about their social customs and tradition. Different kinds of opportunities should be given to them for their development and also for the development of goal of its nation. 'The real test of nationhood is the woman. If the woman has taken her proper place in the society, then the central problem is solved. As the goal of the society really depend upon the unit of the woman. In India, this problem can be solved by bringing upon the woman the sense of responsibility and impressing upon her the divinity and the consciousness of her power and work of motherhood. The work of nation-building must begin from the woman unit. It should be brought to the mind of an Indian woman that she is not a toy, nor a chattel, nor an instrument of pleasure or amusement, but the inspirer of the spirit. Later on she add, that why the names of Sita, Savitri and Damayanti are so sacred and commonplace in every household and remain the cause of inspiration? What are the qualities that made them so great? It was the only spiritual and intellectual development that made them great. It is said in our Sastras, "where women are respected, there the Goddesses are pleased". Women are not so different from one another as man is from another man. Women may form a sisterhood more easily because they are bound to every woman in the world by the common divine quality of motherhood."[15] All these sayings of Sarojini Naidu shows that she want that every woman now should raise themselves to be awaken for their social and political life. They should try to expose themselves to the world about their self-identity and that only could be possible by having the right kind of education. Education is very necessary as to liberate any individual. Educated women could play an important role in the development of a nation.

Sarla Devi Chaudharani (1872-1946)

Sarla Devi was another person in the history of Indian social reformers who worked in the welfare for Indian women. Sarla Devi was one of the architects of a militant mother centred nationalism in the twentieth century. She was one of the very rebellious and independent person. Although she was involved deeply in the different kinds of movement in Bengal, but she worked much to raise consciousness among women for education. Bharat Stree Mahamandal (the Large circle of Indian women) one of the organization of Sarla Devi had its first meeting in Allahabad in 1910. The chief aim of this organisation was to promote female education, that's why, Bharat Stree Mahamandal planned to open branches in different parts of India. 'It developed branches in Lahore, Allahabad, Delhi, Karachi, Amritsar, Hyderabad, Kanpur, Bankura, Hazaribagh, Midnapur and Calcutta, as with the main aim to bring together women of every race, creed, class and party.....On the basis of their common interest in the moral and material progress of the women of India.'[16] The chief aim of the mandal was the spread of female education, apart from this Purdah system and child marriage were considered as the main obstacles to the education of women. These social evils and prejudices makes the woman weaker and somewhere not allowed the woman to take the advantage of education. As it was proposed to let start this organisation in every provinces of India whose main function is to 'collect money and engage teachers who would be sent to the houses of those who desired to educate their wives and daughters. As it was also decided that text-books suitable for teaching Indian women should be written or adapted for the purpose, women should try and enrich the vernacular literature, organise selling centres for women's handicrafts and do what they could to afford medical treatment to women.'[17] This effort of Sarla Devi brought a lot of women to join this organisation. And only women were allowed to join this. Male and female social reformers mentioned above were the iconic figures whenever there is a talk on any issues related to women. Because they really wanted to see women's progress in life. And also wish that they should move forward in life and educate themselves as education is considered an essential part for an individual to move ahead in life.

Now let us discuss some of the persons of United Provinces who showed their keen interest in the progress of women education. These people are not famous as reformers, but here their names are important as they really wanted that their women of India should progress in life.

Lakshmi Sankar Mishra

Lakshmi Sankar Mishra, is one of educational inspectors in the North-Western Provinces. In his note to the education commission of 1882, mainly focused on primary education is very unpopular and defective. And gives solution that to overcome from this defect the ancient Hindu system is needed with certain modification along with the involvement of local boards. He found that primary education is popular as well as has some defects. The natives of these provinces like elementary education, so for this we need to develop the ancient Hindu system.' As matters stand at present, head of the village communities do not care much about the education of their children, and Govt. teacher is not respected by the people as he is considered as a burden. Mostly schools-rooms are generally empty, although the registers of attendance may be full.'[18] Primary education only becomes popular when school management could play an important role, and becomes strict. Teachers appointment must be made at local level and by the board. In this teacher could gain respect by the native people and people also could send their children's freely in the schools.

Mahadevi Verma (1907-87)

'The solution to a problem lies in the knowledge of that problem. And the knowledge expects a seeker. It follows therefore that one desirous of attaining rights should also possess them. Gradually it is this particular characteristics that will be found lacking in the Indian woman.'[19]

The above quotation is of the famous Hindi poet, none another than, Mahadevi Verma from her very famous work, Shrinkhala ki Kadiyan, mainly describes the situation of Indian women who were mainly subjugated and marginalized and also keep ignorant from what they needed. Mahadevi Verma was a well known and a distinguished poet, and renowned essayist of her time, especially she belonged to the twentieth century who frankly took up the women's issues which were publicly debated in the United Provinces much later than in other parts of the country. She was born in Farukhabad in to an educated middle class family and was 'raised under the cultural tutelage of her mother and Westernised and reformist father. And although she was married off at nine, she was yet fortunate enough to continue her studies.'[20] In 1933, she completed her M.A. in Sanskrit from Allahabad University. She understood very well the basis of gender prejudices and socio-cultural suffocation of woman. From her works one can understood the clear image of women all around her. She narrated different and many stories on women, but her one self-narrated real life stories of oppressed woman in her 'Ateet Ke Chal Chitra' work which was very famous at that time. Mahadevi wrote several 'articles between 1931 and 1937, which almost appeared in contemporary women's magazines and in different reputed journals of that time period like 'Chand' and 'Stri Darpan'. These work complied into a volume called titled as 'Shrinkhala Ki Kadiyan' in the year 1931'.[21] Chand and Stri Darpan magazine of that time period considered to be one of the most important, in which mostly women describes about themselves especially about their sacrifices, sorrows which they felt in their life. They express normally their feelings through these journals. Apart as a writer and as a poet, Mahadevi was a social worker too. In 1932, she became the principal of the Prayag Mahila Vidyapeeth. She usually spends her weekends in the villages of Allahabad as to give elementary knowledge and basic teaching about hygiene to rural children. In 1936 she wrote a essay called as 'Our Problems', in which she mainly discuss about the problem of education related to girls. She mainly describes that 'when the structure of intermediary education is erected on the weak and unsteady foundation of primary education, then it is bound to be devoid of durability and utility. When our Indian women will reach up to the intermediary level of education, the special qualities that distinguish them as tend to fade away like morning stars or become rare. What basically defined as higher education either ends up as a source of ultimate dissatisfaction towards life or as the means to acquire necessary desirable things. The real truth is that only two types of women only move forward for higher education. Firstly, one who aspire to have a degree that can enable them to live an independent life like other fellow and second one are those whose goal in life was to use education as to increase their value in the marriage market'[22]. So it can be said that the works of Mahadevi Verma works always encourages woman to move forward in their life as well in educational path also and also led life as independently as don't be depends on others for their future life.

Pandit Tara Datt Gairola

Another person was Pandit Tara Datt Gairola, who is one of the members of Legislative Council of United Provinces. She also expresses views on female education in India. She believed that there are the various factors which are responsible for the backwardness of female education. various factors like early marriages of girls, purdah system, caste prejudices are the major factors which responsible for this. These are the major drawbacks which create obstacles in infusing universal knowledge among the women of India. Later she is of the view that the role of Indian women are different from that of western women. In India the sphere of women is all around her home. It is her whole universe. She was also not allowed to enter in to the economic and political competition with man. Mainly social and domestic service is the special field of her activity. Next obstacles in their educational way is the extreme diversity of races, religious and social condition in India. This makes the general application of one system of education well nigh impossible.[23] It would be now almost impossible to formulate any progress of female education in India, without a thorough examination of all the related difficulties as mentioned above.' I am one of those who believe that the education of women should be entirely in the hands of the community to which they belong. There should be as little Govt. interference as possible'[24]. So person like Tara Chand was always wanted that their female counterparts should be educated and shows their interest in education towards female which were lagging behind in United Provinces.

Saiyid Abdur Raoof

Next is Saiyid Abdur Raoof, Barrister-at-Law at Allahabad. He was also in favour of women education as mentioned in his one of the letter. He say the Govt. was pleased to ask my opinion on the subject of female education in this province while forwarding a copy of the letter no.160, dated the 22nd February, 1916, from the Govt. of India. As he discussed some of the points related to female education. He believes that the high ideal of physical, moral and intellectual improvement of the Indian nation cannot easily be brought home to the masses. If we really want that our female should do progress in their educational life then it is necessary to make them aware about the benefits of having education in their life. The scheme of female education was such so that it could be occupied by any girl of any caste or class. The attempt up to now has been to model female education on the system of the education of boys now prevailing in the country[25]. Curriculum should be same with some slight variations. Boys are generally educated as to get some job, but girls are not educated as accordingly to it. Generally it believes that the system of education which is considered suitable for boys that is not suitable for girls. The motto of education especially for the girls should be to fit them for the sphere of life in which they live. Their education should be of such kind so that they could contribute themselves as useful members of the home and society in which they are living. They should be so educated and trained that they may just become good housewives and good mothers and also ideal members of the society according to the rules of the religion which they prefer and the custom which they follow. According to him, religious and caste prejudice are the greatest hindrances in the progress of female education. He also suggest that special courses of study should be prepared for the girls with due regards to the special needs and requirements of the Special needs and requirements of the special religion and caste to which the girl may belong.[26] He also focused on the Purdah system as one of the stumbling block in the female education. Later he said that if we really want to promote female education in this country then we will have to face this difficulty. And also different measures should be adopted to overcome this difficulty as with the consultation of Govt.

Ajodhya Das

The next name was Ajodhya Das who is Barrister-at-law, also President, Managing Committee of Theosophical Girls School, also recommended some suggestions on female education in one Government's letter dated on 26th June 1916. He is of the view that very little progress was made in female education in this provinces as compared to the provinces of Bombay and Bengal. Govt. also made efforts by opening few schools in the town and districts, which are not very successful. As another reason which is very powerful that the lack of mistress of not proper class with not much of successful personality as a result of which they were not very successful as to inspire parents of the higher classes to send their girls to these institutions. There is also the feeling of hatred against the female education which becoming less with the progress of time. According to him, purdah system, the low marriageable age of girls and mostly general illiteracy are the major stumbling block in the way of the educationist. He later on proposed that schools should be opened in almost every big muhulla with proper furniture and buildings. As to attain the interests of small girls and little children towards education each should be provided with swings and a set of kindergarten materials. System of prizes distribution should be there at least two or three times in a year as to attract more girls and books should be provided free especially to the poorer girls who can't afford it. So, these kinds of the different measures are suggested by Mr. Ajodhya which no longer are recommended by the govt. as to increase the literacy among women and girls.

Miss Booth

Next is, Miss Booth, head of the Gorakhpur branch, Zenana Mission and in charge of five Zenana Mission girls school. She was also of the opinion that progress was very small in the field of women education. There is no fault of the govt. for on making enquiries all round, I find that everything that could be done to educate women, even paying them for it, has been and is still being done.[27] Even she also believes that Purdah system hinders the forward movement and as far as possible reading and writing should be taught by visiting teachers. Another major drawback is the early marriage in the education of women and parents still desiring seclusion for a girl of 11 or 12 and sometimes even at 10 years of age, so zenana teaching should be encouraged.[28] She was in favour of zenana teaching, this will help a lot to women to pay more focus on education. Later she focused that primary education was in more demand among the people as there is a growing desire to include more needle work and knitting in the curriculum of the girls. By knowing this the girls can do small household activities related to them or for others members also. Girls should also taught to learn about the letters. She has another opinion that girls should have more freedom to go schools in the boys so that children of all castes and classes can met together, as this will help them in breaking down the all castes feelings. She also argues that the people of India is not ready to throw off its Purdah yet; when it is, we must have women in front of us who not only can read and write but also have gripped the meaning of womanhood and the dignity of it so as to command respect, and be all that God meant her to be as a woman and a mother.[29]

Raja Chandra Chur Singh

Another one is Hon'ble Raja Chandra Chur Singh of Atra-Chandpur of Raebareli district. As with the reference to your letter (circular) no. 678/XV-85, dated the 29th April, he submitted the brief note on the state of female education in Oudh and also suggested some of the suggestions. He is of the view that the education of respectable Hindu ladies in the city of Lucknow has received late attention and large no. of ladies from good families are educated in the various schools that have been started in the city. In some villages of the Brahmans, Kayasthas and Vaishyas were given certain amount of education to their girls, but among them mostly Brahmin girls are intellectually advanced. With the rapid development in the intellectual progress of male in Oudh, there is a desire for educating the women folk also. At the same time the feeling of Purdah is so strong that even the most highly educated men of the Zamindari families in Oudh are not ready to give it up. If some ladies who have tried to give up Purdah system they are treated more or less as out-castes. Generally it is believed that Purdah was a greater boon to female education in spite of knowing that it is a evil then also it must be kept at all cost. However, it is impossible to expect that many girls of the aristocratic family could be sent to school at present. Later he is of the view of "family classes". Under this system girls would receive education in the house by the head of the family or group of families at fixed hours and go back to their houses in the muhulla after receiving their education. By doing this, even the most conservative parents had no objection of sending their girls to the house of their relative for two or three hours. So, to imply this system a large numbers of teachers are required. Next, he suggested about to start feminine newspapers, as it could be very effective means of educating the respectable ladies as the feminine papers containing useful and interesting articles on biographies of the famous women of the world, some kind of moral lessons, lessons on sanitary environments, cottage industries or some others matters of domestic concern. Apart from this the paper might give selected news about the happenings of the world. At present there is nothing like that, if it will be started it would have a large circulation. So, these are the different recommendations which were given by him to the Govt. of India as to improve the condition of female education in the Provinces. Next is, Hon'ble Rai Ashtbhiya Prasad Bahadur, non-official member of the United Provinces Legislative Council, presented his views towards the education of women and the benefits of education. In general, education, is always beneficial for all individuals. Basically, the illiterateness of them (women) presents a great danger to the social well-being of the Indian communities. It must be very proper to keep the socially upliftment of Indian women. Education in order to be efficient must be suitable, must have a practical value and must be kept progressive to stride side by side with the reform movement culminating in social uplift.[30] Now it would be a new thing for the Govt. to legislate for the betterment of social up-lift of the Indian women. According to him the abolition of Sati and the abolition of irreligious customs of child murders are the two major points in the development of women folk. Later on, widow re-marriage Act was passed by legalising the widow to marry again. Firstly social status of women must be raised then only the attention could be paid on their education system. If we want to run the things smoothly then the social status of the women in India should be raised. The question of the education of boys is still in its first stages. Again he argues that, India is still in her stupor, and the question naturally arises 'Are women of India willing to cast off their prejudices and receive education in its true light, and are they enough in number to be worth the trouble of putting our heads together to lay out schemes even at a time when our attention is wholly taken up the terrible warfare raging on the continent of Europe?'[31]

Let's first create the environment and awareness and also develop very influencing conditions so as to impart education to women in India, and assure them to have benefits of having educated women and profit to them and ourselves too. There is not a proper environment for the benefits of women education in our society. First of all great stress must be laid upon the nature of education which is to be imparted to the girls. According to him, the female education much more depends on the progress of primary education. So, primary education should be made attractive as to enroll more girls. Various kinds of scholarships and prizes should be given in schools liberally. There should be the system of co-education under the supervision of good teachers. The curriculum should be revised with keeping in mind to attract more girls and also to induce their parents to send their girls in school. On the whole their education must be ought to fit them for their position in life, so that they might enjoy a happy, holy life in their homes.

So, on the whole the above mentioned social reformers and different eminent personalities who belongs to U.P. had the same issue as to provide a platform to the women, and to raise their social status. Apart from this the contribution of Arya Samaj also played a major role to uplift the status of women in India. The movement started by Swami Dayanand Saraswati and later taken up by the different leaders evoke a new hope among the people about the development of women education. Basically, the question about the development of women's education was taken up and worked out by the Arya Samaj leaders and members in different parts of N. India. Like the other reforms in the 19th century, this was also started by urban educated elite, in response to the new economic, social and political forces set in motion by colonial rule. The Samaj took up generally different issues related to caste system, untouchability, child marriage etc., but major work done on the development of women education as women were lacking in the field of education. The Samajists felt that Hindu girls needed a special kind of education that would enable them to adapt themselves to the new demands made by the educated men of the family without losing their cultural moorings.[32] Arya Samaj laid the foundation of Dayanand Anglo Vedic (DAV) schools for men and women earlier in Punjab and later spread in many other districts of United Provinces also. People like Devraj, Savitri, Lajjawati, Narayani Devi are the some eminent leaders who gave to women a new definition. They were actively involved in evolving a new concept of women's education. These different people arouse the awareness in United Provinces and in other provinces also. They also collect the fund as to give some help to the institutions of women education in different provinces. Somehow, women's status was altered within the family and the Arya Samaj helped combat urban middle class prejudices against women's education. Although, it can be said that the Arya Samaj movements was intended to "reform" women rather than to reform the social conditions which oppressed them.[33] More women are educated as to get more good educated mothers, wives and daughters. As here this is the brief account of different male and female reformers who time to time took up the different issues related to women. They were the most oppressed one's in the society in every field. The main reasons which are found as by discussing the ideas that the deeply rooted social evils in the society, which were really responsible in degrading the status of women not only in U.P. but in whole India. There are no. of different male and female leaders of different provinces who worked on different women' issues as on female education, child marriage, the observance of Purdah and also the women's status in the family. In fact, they took it too seriously and led many campaigns and movement as related to this. Many of the leaders and poets aroused the feeling of consciousness in the heart and mind of women so that they could raise themselves equally in the home, in society and in nation also.

FOOTNOTES

1. Shodhganga.infilbnet.ac.in/bitstream/10603/20988/7/07_chapter% 202. pdf.accessed on 23/03/2017.
2. Ibid.
3. Ibid.
4. Ibid.
5. Anderson fix Nancy, *Bridging cross cultural feminism: annie beasant and women's rights in England and India, 1874-1933*, women's History review, 3:4, 563-580, DOI; 10.1080/09612029400200070.
6. Ibid.
7. Ibid.
8. S. Bhattacharya (ed.), Document no. 62, from *The Development of Women's Education in India*, pp.316-318.
9. S. Bhattacharya (ed.), Document no.83, p. 387.
10. S. Bhattacharya, Documents no. 69, p. 355.
11. S. Bhattacharya, Document no. 70, pp. 357-358.
12. S. Bhattacharya, Document no. 129, p.516.
13. Ibid., p.358.
14. Sarojini Naidu, Speeches and Writings, 3rd edition, Madras, G.A. Nateson, 1904, pp. 12,13, http://www.archive.org/details/speeches writings of Sarojini Naidu .
15. The 22nd Annual social gathering of the Hindus Ladies Social and Literacy club was held at the Chanda Raniji Hindu Girl's High school, in Bombay, on Sunday the 16th January,1916 as mentioned in Sarojini Naidu, Speeches and Writings, 3rd edition, Madras, G.A. Nateson,

1904,pp.59,60.

16. Geraldine Forbes, Women in Modern India, p.70.
17. Radha Kumar, *The History of doing*, p.39.
18. Sabyasachi Bhattacharya, Document no.53, *Educating the Nation, Documents on the Discourse of National Education in India*,1880-1920.,p.133.
19. Radha Gayatri, *Silent Voices Women's Perceptions about self and Education in Late-Nineteenth century India,* ed. By Parimala V. Rao, p.90.
20. Ibid.,p.102.
21. Ibid.,p.102.
22. Ibid.,p.114.
23. File no. 85 of 1916, Improvement of Female Education, Education Deptt.
24. Ibid.
25. Ibid.
26. Ibid.
27. Ibid.
28. Ibid.
29. Ibid.
30. Ibid.
31. Ibid.
32. Madhu Kishwar, *Arya Samaj and Women's Education Kanya Mahavidyalaya, Jalandhar*, Economic Political Weekly, Vol.XXI, No 17, Review of Women Studies, April 26, 1986, accessed on 11.09.2014.
33. Ibid.

7

Conclusion

Question of women's status has always been a debatable topic as from earlier period till now. Rising the women status from the ancient period till before independence era was taken up by the government, missionaries, social reformers, and other intellectual persons. Every one was concerned about rebooting the status of women in India. The 'status' word here include viz., progress in socio-economic status, and also progress in educational status. One of the remarkable progress in India was the awakening of Indian Womanhood among the women of India, which had been forging from the past hundred years. Modern women enjoy a modicum of equality within the society and also within the nation. But this whole history of this new woman was filled with lots of aggressions, lots of difficulties, lots of efforts from the different eminent leaders.

Now, before describing the new woman of free India, lets look into the historical background of the Indian society from earlier times till the arrival of the British. As it was discussed in the Introduction chapter, that women's image in earlier phase, was totally an ideal image for all. As women of earlier time was highly qualified and very intellectual in every field. Women in Vedic times enjoyed equal status as compared to man. She enjoyed full rights over everything. She also acquired higher education to have any kind of intellectual debate with anyone. As in case of marriage also she had full rights over this. She could choose her life partner of her own choices. Women had full freedom during ancient time. This freedom gets lower in the medieval period when lot of restrictions were imposed over them and did not give any attention to women's education. This was the time when the condition and status of women got lowered and continued till up to the advent of British on the Indian subcontinent.

As in the context of social status also, women suffered a lot and it was most deplorable condition in United Provinces. As mentioned earlier that in earlier time they were respected and no cruel evils occurred at that time. But later on most of evils took cruel shape during later years as revealed by different sources and historians. Different social customs and prejudices occurred in 18th century in India. These social evils lowered the status of women, who mainly lost respect in the society which was there in ancient time.

The various social evils like Purdah system, Child marriage, female infanticide, female foeticide, sati system and most importantly the patriarchal nature of society are responsible for the lower status of women in Indian society. They are the major obstacles and stumbling blocks in the progress of women education not only in United Provinces but also in whole of India. It was there in every nook and corner of the country. No doubt it affected the literacy rate in the provinces. It took a lot of time to get rid from these evils. Actually before Independence, literacy was very low in the provinces and United Provinces which is the most backward among all provinces. One of the reasons seems to be the social evils, which normally don't allow the women to pursue education at higher level, and also restricted them to move in the society. These social evils were so much deeply rooted in the society that they could not overcome from this. Among these evils, Sati came to be one of the most practiced customs in the different parts of the provinces. It was most cruel type of evil. As women get burned themselves alive on the funeral pyre of their husbands. Sometime it was carried out forcefully by the people of the society. It was one of the horrible practices which were prevalent in the United Provinces also. People held the view that without husband a woman had nothing to do in the society so it's better to give her life. They are considered as burden to the family. Sometime it led to child widows in very little age and also lost opportunity from education at very early age they had to devoid themselves from all social happiness of their life. They were so disrespected in the society as no attention was paid towards her education. Education was considered as a sin for girls child during colonial period. They lost their freedom by so much of seclusion, early marriage and also due to other reasons which affected their life and had a bad impact on their education system also. These social evils discriminated against women in every walk of life in the society.

All these evils were not very fruitful to women's life. Again one of the evil called Purdah System also kept women in seclusion in all respects. It keeps away them from education. It emerged in medieval times and later on it was practiced in different parts of India, and also in Oudh region. It is clear that all these evils created hurdles in women life as in education also. Like this, one more evil Female Infanticide or female Foeticide also created difficulties in women's life. Female infanticide was one of the cruel evils in the provinces, and also one of the stumbling blocks in the way of women education. Above all these things, the so called Patriarchal nature of society was also one of the reasons for the backwardness of Indian women especially in Northern India. Patriarchal nature mainly lowers down the status of women in the society. It was more famous in northern India. As the word 'patriarchy' defines the ruling of men power in the family. It was men who basically take all decisions related to anything even related to women life also. These evils gave them no opportunity for education in life. No doubt it took a long time to break this chain of social evils from the society and also from the heart of men counter parts of the family who never thought good for women, who always treated her as an object for sexual pleasure. Women took a long time to be independent even to march forward in their life and to take decisions by their own restriction on women and seclusion had a negative impact on the education of women. These are the hurdles of their life, which mainly stops them to march forward in their life. These evils no doubt already destroyed the status of women in the society, and to recover this image it will take a long time to bring about equality between men and women.

Therefore, these are the different difficulties towards the progress of Women education in the United Provinces. Progress of women or education of women was not an easy task for the British. To maintain the same was not as easy task for any one. One of the Frenchman said that the best way to judge the position of a nation was to find out the status of its women. These lines seem to be correct and true. As no nation can develop without the progress of its half population leaving as illiterate and uneducated.

At the beginning of colonial time, the East India Company paid less or little attention towards education. It was almost negligible in the context of women. As EIC did not consider it necessary to educate Indian people. By passing the Charter Act of 1813, EIC forcefully accepted the responsibility of education. It was decided that one lakh rupees would be granted every year for education. And from it very small amount of money were spent on women education which not fulfilling the demand of women education in the provinces. Later on Maculay Minutes of 1835 and Wood's Despatch of 1854 put their focus and efforts on the issue of women education. But not much could be attained, until in 1882 when the IEC came out with new provisions and also with minute difficulties in the progress of women education in every province. It made up what was lacking in the Wood's Despatch by various provisions.

Up to 1882, there were only 17 schools in NWP and Oudh provinces. No doubt these numbers were too small to describe the progress of women education in the provinces. It took time to develop it more in numbers. But later on in different provinces like, Agra, Kanpur, Muttra and Mynpoorie some more govt. schools were opened keeping in view the development of women's education. Progress in women education was not an easy task for govt. as they were subjected to social evils in this era. IEC of 1882, created a new hope in this direction, and also more in favour of women education. The commission was asked to pay more attention on primary education which was totally neglected in the provinces, because of one evil called child marriage, which was highly prevalent at that time in the provinces. Oudh was lagging behind in this matter. EC of 1882 very briefly observed the problems of women and also recommended several solutions as to enhance the women education in total. IEC of 1882 recommended that focus should be on primary and secondary level of education. Different systems of grant-in-aid were also recommends by it. It also recommended the proper text-books for the suitability according to girls. Different types of scholarships and prize distribution system was launched as to attract more girls towards the schools for education in India. Time to time all these recommendations were implemented in different sections of the provinces, somewhere met with success and somewhere failure. Different schools were opened by govt. in the provinces. It's true that NWP and Oudh was lagging behind in terms of girls education as compared to others provinces, as mainly revealed by different reports. But later on with the efforts of govt. and other highly intellectual persons women education started developing gradually. In fact, now women education gained the first place for consideration in all different schemes which were initiated.

Provisions of Compulsory Primary Education scheme was also launched. In the beginning it was meant for boys, but later on implemented for girls also. United Provinces District Boards Primary Education Act of 1926, brought certain changes in many district regarding primary education. Different provinces showed positive results in the context of boys as well as in girls case. Girls were also progressing activity in secondary schools also. Govt. efforts were not up to the mark regarding women education as in secondary schools also. But with the help of others agencies girls education was doing better. Some progress could be seen in girls education, by passing different regulations and somehow applying it. One of the other drawback in girls education that insufficient supply of lady teachers and lady inspectress in majority of govt. schools and without proper curriculum in girls schools. These seemed to be the major drawback in govt. schools. These were considered the main hurdles in girls education in United Provinces. People of the provinces were sacred to send their daughters alone in the schools, as there were more male staff in girls schools. This restricted parents also. Education was there, but restricted up to the higher class of the society, measures were also taken to uplift the lower sections but could not achieve much.

Apart from the govt. efforts to educate women, role of Christian Missionaries coud not be neglected. They were the pioneers in the field of women education not only in United Provinces, but in whole of India. The missionaries came to Indian sub-continent, merely to fulfill their evangelical agenda and also to convert the native people. But gradually they pursued the social services and fully devoted their lives and service to native population. They had their valuable contributions in the field of education and health. Their serious dedication in the field of education is one of the most striking things of the missionaries. Earlier they had only the view of conversion of the people, but later on they took their interest in the field of education and especially for women education.

Basically, missionary societies started entering India after the renewal of EIC, in 1813. From this time period onwards they got permission to continue their activities in the company's administered areas. It was in 1833 that the missionaries of various countries also got the permission to enter in the Indian Peninsula. Later, on in 1854 trough the Wood's Despatch they got another chance to strengthen its position. In contrast to this, the outlining of this despatch mainly helped the missionaries again to hold a strong footing in the educational terrain of India. When missionaries entered into this field, the govt.'s started withdrawing from the field of education.

The Indian Education Commission of 1882 mainly helped the various private agencies who worked for the cause of women education in different provinces. In fact, it also recommended the system of grant-in-aid to encourage the various private bodies in this field. As well as the various Christian missionary societies got help from the govt. as to promote female education in different provinces in which they were mainly lacking. The missionaries decided to establish a large network of missionary schools, throughout the provinces, which mainly filled the gap, after govt.'s withdrawal from the field.

The initiation of women education was taken by missionaries in United Provinces. They don't discriminate people on basis of caste, creed and community. The CMS, LMS, SPG, CMD were the important missionary societies who were involved in teaching and helped high schools and colleges across the major portion of north India. The societies who involved in NWP of Agra and Oudh (later United Provinces) were CMS, LMS, and SPG mostly active.

Methods of instructions of missionaries were very simple and mostly understood by the local people. Apart from spreading the knowledge of Bible they also focused on vernacular language. They launched the scheme of day school, also by establishing orphanages, and most important by opening the system of Zenana teaching, which became most populous in every part of India. There were numerous schools and colleges which were established by missionaries and the result was that they were larger in numbers as compared to govt. schools and colleges, and also had more pupils than govt. schools. Missionaries grant were also very high as compared to others. They got some grant from govt., some from other highly rich zamindars and local people who became interested in women education. Some intellectual people and some zamindars of different provinces granted some land and rupees for the establishing of more girls schools and colleges in their areas. Missionary Schools had missionary ladies for visiting schools and keep an eye over daily experiments and also gave daily reports. All this system was lacking in govt. schools as they had insufficient lady staff and lady inspectresses. No doubt the efforts of missionaries were fruitful for the people of Oudh (United Provinces) which can be visible by increasing no. of schools for the people of provinces. One of the person called Mr. Reuther, opened two or three schools for girls in the Fyzabad city. With passage of time people started recognizing the advantages of having educated women in the society. As many numerous people showed their interest in female education. By watching the interest of missionaries in women education other people also got awareness in this direction. Females of every class getting interested towards Zenana teaching, which was started by missionaries. They now started showing their keen interest in learning basic knowledge. During 19th century, and later on various missionaries or aided schools were opened for the people of United Provinces in various district like Agra, Allahabad, Benaras for the promotion of female education. Mission schools were making their efforts for female education and more schools were opened at primary, secondary and higher level. In context of higher education, the IT college of Lucknow was the most important and reputed among all. It was maintained by none another than missionaries and funded by them. They released grant for it. As for text- books and curriculum, they made it according to the suitability of native girls. English as a subject was made compulsory at primary and at secondary level, so that people could have the basic knowledge.

Besides, the missionaries, the social reformers also who took up the cause of women education and also to enhance the women status in the society so that they can have their own identity. Social reformers played an important part in getting rid of different social evils which was there from so many decade. Both male and female reformers took up the different issues and helped it in getting away from it. They uplifted women socially, economically, and politically in India. The main aim of reformers is to create equality between both the sexes. The reformers on global level like Raja Ram Mohan Roy, Annie Beasent, Pandita Ramabai, Lala Lajpat Rai, Gopal Krishna Gokhale, Sarojini Naidu, Sarla Devi Chaudharani, Mahadevi Verma etc., are some of the most prominent leaders who helped in raising the status of women on global level by opposing different social evils which was frequently followed in the society and also by opening different schools and colleges for women education. Nevertheless, the name of Nehru, Gandhi, and Ambedkar can't be forgotten in terms of promotion of women education in independent India. They worked for enhancement of women's life and also to uplift their status in the society so that they can be respected and move ahead in their life.

Apart from these reformers there also some of the reformers or we can say the people both official and intellectual persons of United Provinces, who contributed their ideas and passed different regulations for the growth of women education of the provinces. These persons are Pandit Tara Datt Gairola, Saiyid Abdur Raoof, Mr. Ajodhya Das, Miss Booth, Hon'ble Raja Chandra Chur Singh, and many more intellectual people who promoted female education in United Provinces. They also discussed about their difficulties and also remedies and also created an awareness among the native people about the benefits of women education. Swami Dayanad Saraswati founder of Arya Samaj of Northern India played an important role to encourage women education and also helps in removing different evils like child marriage, dowry, polygamy and many more which degrated the women status and lowered the education in United provinces.

Therefore, from the above discussion it can be said that at the beginning of the British rule, women education was mainly lower in NWP and Oudh (later United Provinces). But with passage of time with different recommendation and also by the efforts of Govt., Missionaries, different social reformers and others intellectual persons, female education got fillip and it led to the development of literacy among women. Growth of Female education in United Provinces was achieved by mainly four groups: the British, Missionaries Pioneers, Indian male reformers and by educated Indian Women.

Appendices

Appendix I

Indian Education Commission or Hunter Commission of 1882

Recommendations are as following of this particular Commission:

1. That female education be treated as a legitimate charge alike on Local, on Municipal, and on Provincial Funds, and receive special encouragement.
2. That all female schools or orphanages, whether on a religious basis or not be eligible for aid so far they produce any secular results, such as a knowledge of reading or of writing.
3. That the conditions of aid to girls' schools be easier than to boys' schools, and the rates higher–more especially in the case of those established for poor or low-caste girls.
4. That the rules for grants be so framed as to allow for the fact that girl's schools generally contain a large proportion of beginners, and of those who cannot attend school for so many hours a day, or with such regularity, as boys.
5. That the standards of instruction for primary girls' schools be simpler than those for boy's schools, and be drawn up with special references to the requirements of home life, and to the occupations open to women.

6. That the greatest care be exercised in the selection of suitable text-books for girls' schools, and that the preparations of such books be debarred from a grant on account of its not leving fees.
7. That, while fees be levied where practicable no girls' schools be debarred from a grant on account of its not leving fees.
8. That special provision be made for girls' scholarships, to be awarded after examination, and that, with a view to encouraging girls to remain longer at school, a certain proportion of them be reserved for girls not under twelve years of age.
9. That liberal aid be offered for the established, in suitable localities, of girls' schools in which English should be taught in addition to the vernacular.
10. That special aid be given, where necessary, to girls' schools that make provisions for boarders.
11. That the various Department of Public Instruction be requested to arrange, in concert with managers of girls' schools, for the revision of the code of Rules for grants-in-aid in accordance with the above Recommendations.
12. That, as mixed schools, other than infant schools, are not generally suited to the conditions of this country, the attendance of girls at boys' schools be not encouraged, except in places where girls' schools cannot be maintained.
13. That the establishment of infant schools or classes, under schoolmistresses, be liberally encouraged.
14. That female schools be not placed under the management of Local boards or of Municipalities unless they express a wish to take charge of them.
15. That the first appointment of schoolmistresses in girls' schools under the management of Municipal or Local Boards be left to such Boards, with the proviso that the mistress be either certificated, or approved by the Department by the Boards, subject to the approval of the Department.

16. That rules be framed to promote the gradual supersession of male by female teachers in all girls' school.
17. That, in schools under female teachers, stipendiary pupil-teacherships be generally encouraged.
18. That the attention of local Governments be invited to the question of establishing additional Normal schools or classes; and that those under private management receive aid, part of which might take the form of a bonus for every pupil passing the certificate examinations.
19. That the department certificate examinations foe teachers be open to all candidates, wherever prepared.
20. That teachers in schools for general education be encouraged by special rewards to prepare pupils for examinations for teachers' certificate, and that girls be encouraged by the offer of prizes to qualify for such certificates.
21. That, in Districts where Europeans or Eurasian young women are required as teachers in native schools, special encouragement be given to them to qualify in a vernacular language.
22. That liberal inducements be offered to the wives of schoolmasters to qualify as teachers and that in suitable cases widows be trained as schoolmistress, care being taken to provide them with sufficient protection in the places where they are to be employed as teachers.
23. That grants for zenana teaching be recognised as a proper charge on public funds, and be given rules which will enable the agencies engaged in that work to obtain substantial aid for such secular teaching as may be tested by an inspectress, or other female agency.
24. That associations for the promotion of female education, by examinations or otherwise, be recognised by the Department, and encouraged by grants under suitable conditions.
25. That female inspecting agency be regarded as essential to the full development of female education, and be more largely employed than hitherto.

26. That an alternative examination in subjects suitable for girls be established in standard to the Matriculation examination, but having no relation to any existing University course.
27. That endeavors be made to secure the services of native gentlemen interested in female education on committees for the supervision of girls' schools, and that European and native ladies also be invited to assist such committees.

Appendix II

Speech Delivered by Mr. Chamberlain to the Deputation on Female Education in India on 12th October 1915

Mrs. Fawcett, Ladies and Gentlemen,

Let me say, in the first place, how glad I am that this Deputation should have been introduced by Mrs. Fawcett. It would be almost an impertinence in me to express my sense of the many reasons she has for her great interest in India, and of her right to speak on anything that concerns women.

I have listened, Ladies and Gentlemen, with interest to all that you have said.. I do not think is any difference between us as to the importance of women's education in India. There are some differences, I think, and I am going to deal quite frankly with them before I sit down, but as to importance of the study of women's education in India, and of gradually providing better facilities for that education, there is no difference between you and me. I think it was Sir Krishna that women in India had less influence on the life of the people of the country than elsewhere. I do not think any wise man would underrate the influence of women in any community may be, to suppose that the Government of India were indifferent to the subject or unconscious of its importance, it is not as if there were any reason to suppose that they underrate it. On the contrary, we have every reason to know that they realize its magnitude and are impressed with how much remains to be done; and under these circumstances I think that you ought to be satisfied if I say that I will submit Government of India for their consideration, but that I shall ot make any recommendation upon it, nor should I feel that I was justified in appointing a Committee of Enquiry over their heads. When it is possible to make progress I hope that some of the facts in the resolution on the Government of India, on which you, in your speeches, have laid stress, will be borne in mind. After all, the education of women, in the sense in which you now speak of it, is a very modern development even in the Western world. Even here, we have by no means satisfactory solved all the problems which it opens up, and I hope that whatever authorities have to deal with this question in India will not hastily assume that the needs of is, after all, only partially successful here, and in some respects is still to be regarded in the light of an experiment.

I have had the opportunity of reading a report which was the outcome of the enquiry by Sir Dorabji Tata, to which Mr. Jusuf Ali referred. I have found it a very interesting account of the state of things which the lady appointed by she made her visit to India. I venture to draw one conclusion from it here, that you cannot learn very much at this moment in regard to education–and especially female education in India–from statistics. You cannot carry your conclusions very far from a mere examination of the number of girls who attend school per 100,000 of the population in one Province or another. There are special circumstances in each province to be taken into account. But it is not only that. When they get to school, it does not follow that they are being educated in any real sense of the world. I think that after the creation of a desire by the Indians themselves for increased facilities for women's education, the first necessity is for better trained teachers, and I think I must add, better paid teachers, for you cannot get the right sort at the salaries which are frequently or generally offered. I think those who laid stress on that really put thier fingers on the point at which progress has got to begin. It is n good in my opinion– I speak after a very short experiences–starting out, as one speaker said, with " a large scheme" which would sweep a number of girls into schools, unless you have a staff who are capable of training them.

Ladies and Gentlemen, I need not detain you any longer, I am not unsympathetic–I hope that nothing I have said will cause you think I am unsympathetic–with those Indians who feel that the future of their country must largely depend upon the satisfactory progress of women's education in that country. I am not unsympathetic to that point of view, but I cannot pretend to think that the particular moment you have chosen to address me is happy one, nor that I believe it would be wise to consider that question now, and I leave with you, as my last word, my opinion that a movement of this kind must begin in India, if it is to have reasonable prospects of success and I must add that, opportunities having been given to Indian opinion to express itself, there can be no reason for us not to look to India itself for help.

Appendix III

The United Provinces District Boards Primary Education Act, 1926

United Provinces Act No. 1 of 1926.

(Passed by the Local Legislature of the United Provinces of Agra and Oudh.)

Received the assent of the Governor of the United Provinces of Agra and Oudh on March 23, 1926, and of the Governor-General on April 21, 1926, and was published under section 81 of the Government of India Act on May 8, 1926.

An act to provide for the extension of primary education in rural areas under district boards in the United Provinces.

Whereas it is the declared policy of the Government of the United Provinces that universal, free and complusory primary education for boys and girls should be reached by a definite programme of progressive expansion and whereas it is expedient to provide for a progressive development and expansion of primary education; it is hereby enacted as follows:–

1. (1) This Act may be called the United Provinces District Boards Primary Education Act, 1926.

(2) it extends to all the areas under the jurisdiction of the district boards in the United Provinces.

(3) It shall be constructed as supplementary to the United Provinces District Boards Act, 1922, hereinafter called the Principal Act.

2. In this Act, unless there is anything repugnant in the subject or context–

(1) "to attend" a recognised primary school means to be present for instruction at such school, on such days in the year, at such time or times, and for so many hours on each day of attendance, as may be fixed by the board;

(2) "child" means a child whose age is not less than six and not more than eleven years: provided that "child", when referring to a Muslim girl, shall mean a child whose age is not less than five and not more than nine years

(3) "parent" includes a guardian or any person who has the actual custody or is in charge of a child;

(4) "primary education" means instruction in reading, writing and arithmetic of such standard as may be prescribed for primary schools by the local government and such instruction, in other subjects, if any, as may be determined by the board with the approval of the prescribed authority;

(5) "recognized primary school" includes a school or a department of a school in which instruction in primary education is given and which is for the time being recognized by the Director of Public Instruction;

(6) "school committee" means a committee appointed under the provisions of section 6 of this Act;

(7) "school area" means the area within a radius of one mile by the nearest route from a primary school maintained by the board and included within the local limits of a board;

(8) "tahsil area" means the area comprised in a tahsil and included within the local limits of a board;

(9) "thana area" means the area comprised in the limits of a police station and included within the local limits of a board;

(10) "village area" means the area comprised in a village.

3. (1) On the application of the board the local government may declare, by notification, that the primary education of male children shall be compulsory in the whole of the board, issue a notification that the primary education of female children shall be compulsory in the whole or any part of such area.

(2) Where a notification issued under subsection (1) is in force in any area, the local government may, on the application of the board, issue a notification that the primary education of female children shall be compulsory in the whole or any part of such area.

(3) A notification issued under this section shall specify the date from which, and the area or areas in which primary education shall be compulsory, and public notice shall be given of the notification locally in the area or areas concerned.

(4) A board, if called upon by the local government so to, shall within a time to be specified by the local government submit a scheme to provide compulsory primary education in such area as the local government may direct and in the case of children of either sex or both sexes as the local government may specify.

(5) If a board when called upon makes default in submitting a scheme or after a scheme has been sanctioned omits to make adequate provision for compulsory education in accordance with a scheme as sanctioned or to bring into operation or to continue to keep in operation such scheme, the local government my after due inquiry appoint a person to submit the scheme or to bring it into operation or to continue to keep it in operation as the case may be and the expense there of shall be paid by the board to the local government may make an order directing any person who has, for the time being, custody of any moneys on behalf

as he may have in his hands or may from time to time receive and such person shall be bound to obey such order.

4. A notification shall not be issued under section 3 unless (a) the board has by special resolution which has been passed by a vote of not less than one-half of the total number of members constituting the board, resolved that such primary education should be made compulsory, and (b) the local government is satisfied that the board is in a position to make, and will make adequate provision in recognized primary schools for such compulsory primary education free of charge.

5. An application by the board under section 3 shall be made in such manner s may be prescribed by the local government and the board shall furnish such information in respect of the application as may be required by the local government.

6. (1) Where a notification has been issued under section 3, the board shall appoint one or more committees for the purpose of exercising the powers and performing the duties of the school committee under this Act.

   (2) It shall be the duty of such school committee, subject to the provisions of the this Act, to enforce the provisions of this act respecting the attendance of children at school and the employment of children.

7. Where a notification under section 3 is in force in any area, the parent of every child to whom the notification applies shall, if such child ordinarily resides in such area, in the absence of a reasonable excuse as hereinafter defined, cause such child to attend a recognized primary school.

8. Any of the following circumstances shall be deemed to be a reasonable excuse within the meaning of section 7–

   (1) that there is no accommodation in a recognized primary school within a distance to be fixed by the school committee and measured according to the nearest route from the residence of the child;

   (2) that the child has been exempted by the school committee on religious grounds;

(3) that the child is receiving otherwise than in a recognized primary school primary education in a satisfactory manner;

(4) that the child is certified by such authority as may be appointed in this behalf by the board to have completed the primary course;

(5) that the child has been granted temporary leave of absence from school, in accordance with regulations made under this Act by the board;

(6) that the child is certified by a medical officer approved for this purpose by the board to be unfit to attend school by reason of some bodily defect or infirmity;

(7) that the child has, with the consent of the prescribed authority, been exempted by the school committee for special reasons recorded by it in writing.

9. Where the school committee is satisfied that a parent who is bound under the provisions of section 7 to cause a child to attend a recognized primary school, has failed to do so, the school committee after giving the parent an opportunity of being heard, and after such inquiry as it considers necessary, may pass an order directing the parent to cause such child to attend a recognized primary school from a date which shall be specified in the order.

10. (1) Any parent against whom an order has been passed under section 9, and who without reasonable excuse as defined in section 8 has failed to obey such order, shall on conviction before a magistrate be liable to a fine not exceeding five rupees.

(2) Any parent who having been convicted of an offence under sub- section (1) continues to disobey the order passed under section 9 shall be liable to a further fine not exceeding one rupee for every day, after the date of the first conviction, during which he is proved in a subsequent proceeding taken before a magistrate to have persisted in disobeying the order.

11. Any person other than the parent who, during the prescribed hours of attendance at school, utilizes on his own behalf or on

behalf of any other person, in connexion with any employment, whether for remuneration or not, the services of any child whose parent is required under this act to cause him to attend a recognized primary school, shall, on conviction before a magistrate, be liable to a fine not exceeding twenty-five rupees.

12. (1) No court shall take cognizance of an offence under section 10 or section 11 except o the complaint of or on information received from the school committee, or from such person as may be authorized by the school committee by general or special order in this behalf:

Provided that the school committee or the person authorized in this behalf shall before instituting a prosecution against any person cause a warning to be given to him in writing.

(2) The school committee or the person authorized in this behalf may, instead of instituting or continuing a prosecution for an offence, compound the same on the payment by the person accused of such offence of such sum as it deems proper not exceeding the amount is punishable under this Act.

13. The local government, after taking into consideration any views expressed by the board in this behalf, may, by notification, exempt any particular class or community from the operation of this Act.

14. No fee for primary education shall be charged in respect of any child compulsory attending a recognized primary school within an area in which a notification under section 3 is in force.

15. All sums realized on conviction or by way of composition under the provisions of this Act shall be credited to the board's fund.

16. When the local Government is of opinion that default has been made by any board in respect of its duties under this Act, it may, after giving the board an opportunity of furnishing an explanation, cancel the notification issued under section 3.

17. (1) The local Government may, after previous publication, make rules for carrying out the purposes of this Act.

(2) In particular and without prejudice to the generality of the power conferred by sub- section (1), the local government may make rules–

(a) prescribing the authorities mentioned in clause (4) of section 2 and clause (7) of section 8;

(b) prescribing under clause (4) of section 2 the standard of instruction in primary schools;

(c) prescribing the manner in which application may be made by the particulars to be stated in such application;

(d) determining generally what shall be considered to be adequate provision for compulsory primary education free of charge;

(e) requiring the boards to prepare and publish a register of children in the whole or in ant part of the board's area;

(f) defining the condition on which the local government will bear a share of the cost of providing primary education;

(g) requiring the board to submit such returns as the local government may think fit showing the action taken and progress made by the board under this act; and

(h) laying down the conditions of and qualifications for the appointment of teachers with due regard to the appointment of teachers with due regard to the educational needs of different communities in every locality.

18. With the preivous sanction of the local Government a board in the area of which a notification under section 3 is in force may this Act, prescribing–

(a) the supply of text-books and educational requisites to the children of indigent parents free of charge;

(b) the manner in which the school committee shall be constituted, its jurisdiction, the number of its members, and their duties, powers and responsibilities;

(c) the steps which the school committee may take to secure the attendance of children at school, and the conditions under which leave of absence

Appendix IV

List of Graphs

Figure showing literate male and female in each provinces of the year 1914-15.

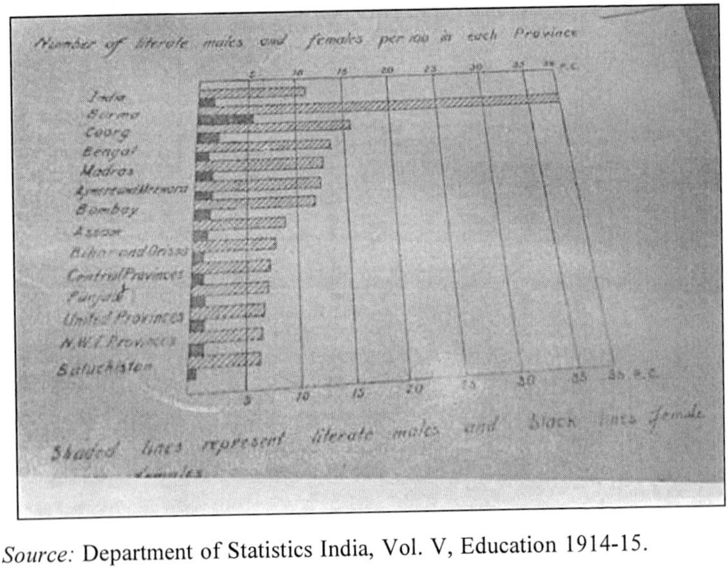

Source: Department of Statistics India, Vol. V, Education 1914-15.

Figure showing number of pupils in all institutions in India, 1916.

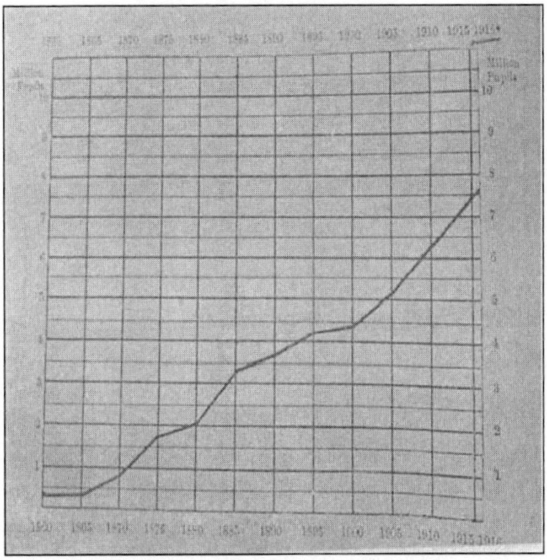

Source: Department of Statistics India , Vol. V Education, 1915-16.

Figure shows the expenditure on education in India, 1916.

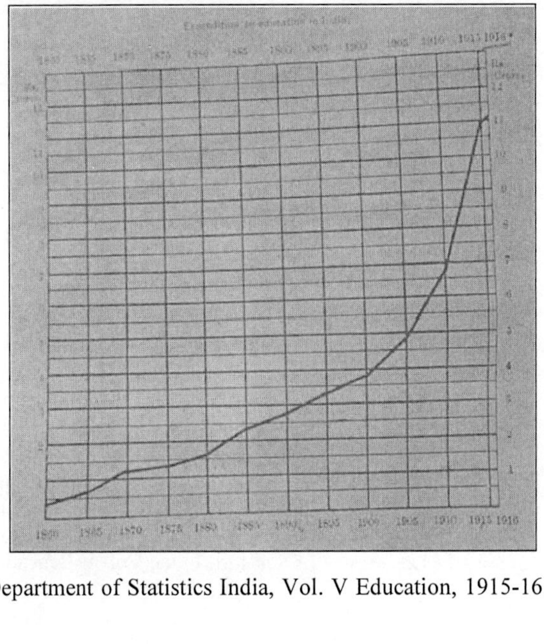

Source: Department of Statistics India, Vol. V Education, 1915-16.

Figures shows the no. of Pupils in all institutions and expenditure on education in India, 1917.

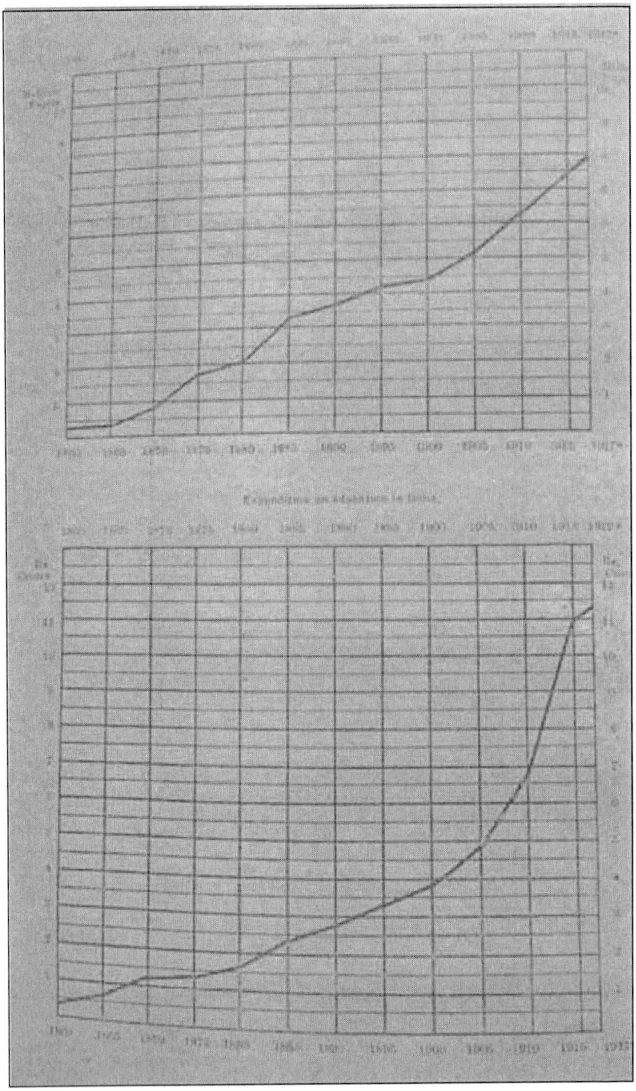

Source: 10th Issue of Department of Statistics India, Vol. V Education 1916-17.

Figure shows the Literacy in various district of United Provinces, 1921.

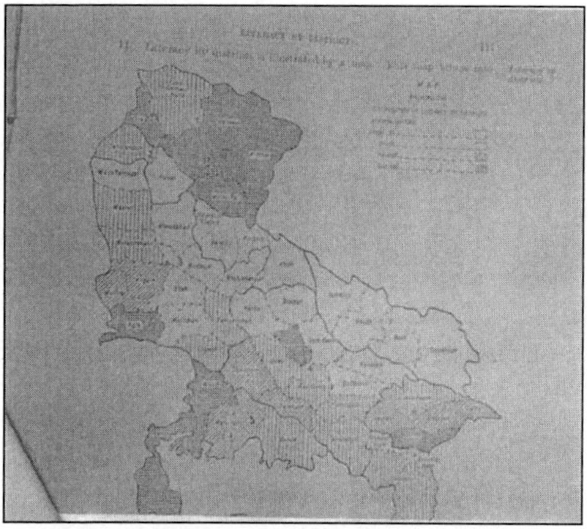

Source: Census of 1921 of United Provinces of Agra and Oudh.

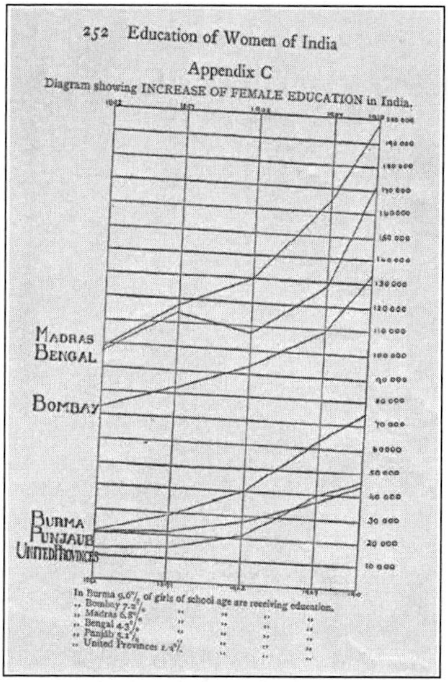

Source: Cowan, Minna G., The Education of The Women of India–Primary Source Edition.

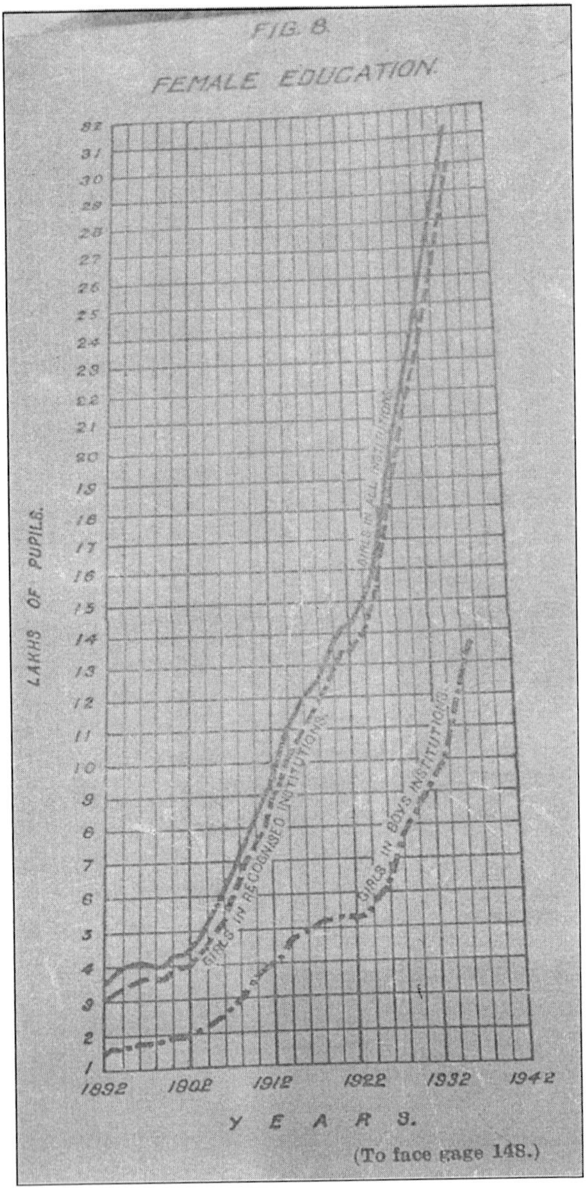

Source: John Sargent, Progress of Education in India, 1932-37.

Source: IT College Lucknow Administrative Report of United Provinces 1923-24

Annie Besant

Raja Ram Mohan Roy, Great Indian Social Reformer

Savitri Bai Phule, First Woman Teacher of India.

Bibliography

Primary Sources

Records at the Uttar Pradesh State Archives

File no. 3/1887	Report of The Indian Education Commission.
File no. 34/1887	Vocations in Govt. schools and colleges of the NWP and Oudh.
File no. 40/1884	Code of Regulations for European Schools NWP and Oudh.
File no. 45/1887	Annual report on Public Instruction in the NWP and Oudh.
File no. 191/1890	Extension of the Central Normal School at Lucknow.
File no. 218/1890	La Martinire College trust funds, Lucknow Branch.
File 81/1896	Grant-in-aid to Vernacular Primary Schools in NWP and Oudh.
File no. 122/1898	Jubliee High School, Lucknow.
File no. 45/1908	La Martinier College, Lucknow.
File no. 58/1908	Reorganisation of the Inspecting Agency of Anglo-Vernacular Girls Schools.

File no. 61/1908	Education Code for the United Provinces.
File no.62/1908	Grant-in-aid to Canning college Lucknow.
File no. 66/1908	Canning College Fund Lucknow.
File no. 79/1908	Appointment of M.G. Gardner Brown to the Indian Education Services.
File no. 80/1908	Establishment of Govt. High schools in the United Provinces.
File no. 138/1908	General Improvement of Secondary Education.
File no. 151/1908	Jubliee High school, Lucknow.
File no. 154/1908	Improvement of Female Education.
File no. 184/1908	Appointment of Miss. H.G. Stuart as Chief Inspectress of Girls Schools.
File no. 193/1908	Schemes for encouraging the wives and female relatives of school masters.
File no. 235/1908	Religious education in Govt. schools.
File no. 259/1908	Huisainabad High school, Lko.
File no. 269/ 1908	Normal Schools for girls, Lko.
File no. 292/1908	Appointment of Mr. S.G. Dunn to the Indian Education Service.
File no. 299/1908	Appointment of Mr. E. Stokes to the Indian Education Services.
File no. 303/1908	Appointment of Mr. H. Bamister B.Sc. to the Indian services.
File no. 327/1908	Appointment of Mr. A.H. Mackenzie.
File no. 336/1908	Colvin School, Lko.
File no. 375/1908	Girls Model School.
File no. 177/1909	Lady Hewett Scholarship Endowment trust, Raebarellie.
File no. 259/1909	Question of making the post of female teachers in girls model schools on Rs. 15 per mensem.
File no. 13/1910	Ross Scholarship endowment trust, Gonda.
File no. 175/1909	Indian Christian Academy at Allahabad.

File no. 52/1910	Payment of Conveyance charges to teachers of girls schools in Lko. Attending the special classes at girls normal school.
File no. 284/1910	Bhaiya Jang Bahadur Singh Scholarship, Gonda.
File no. 382/1910	Vernacular Education in school.
File no. 48/1911	Causes of the set-back to primary education.
File no. 198/1911	Proposal to make elementary education free in all govt. board, municipal and aided school.
File no. 261/1911	Queen Victoria Memorial Fund Cawnpore.
File no. 2/1912	Grant to the Kalicharan High School, Lko.
File no. 38/1912	Imperial grant for the extension and improvement of primary education in the United Provinces.
File no. 11/1912	System of grant-in-aids for primary schools for Indians.
File no. 177/1912	Model girls schools in United Provinces.
File no. 299/1912	Three years programme of requirement for female education.
File no. 344/1912	Colvin School, Lko.
File no. 95/1912,	Proposal to prohibit teaching of English below Class iii in recognised Anglo–Vernacular schools for girls.
File no. 98/1913	Educational Policy of Govt. of India.
File no. 135A/1913	Primary Education.
File no. 469/1913	Establishment of Ist grand aided College at Gorakhpur.
File no. 138/1914	Training of female teachers for India.
File no. 141/1914	Isabella Thoborn College, Lko.
File no. 85/1916	Improvement of female education.
File no. 7/1918	Establishment of a Shia College at Lko.
File no.45/1919	Rules under section 18, United Provinces Primary Education Act, 1919.
File no. 56/1921	Isabella Thoborn College, Lko.

File no. 584/1921	Proceeding of the meeting of the Women's Education Committee.
File no. 50/1921	Report on Female Education.
File no. 979/1921	Compulsory Primary Education in Cawnpore municipality.
File no. 725/1923	Compulsory Primary Education in Unnao municipality.
File no. 762/1923	Compulsory Education in Sitapur municipality.
File no. 802/1925	Compulsory Primary Education in Lakhimpur municipality.
File no. 1020/1925	United Provinces district boards Primary Education Act, 1926.
File no. 1024/1925	Mr. Kichlu's Report on improvement and expansion of primary education.
File no. 1072/1925	Primary education in the whole city of Lucknow municipality.
File no. 1176/1927	Control over grant-in-aid to local bodies.
File no. 1183/1927	Compulsory Education in Sitapur municipality.
File no. 1184/1927	Compulsory Education in Lakhimpur municipality.
File no. 1198/1927	Compulsory Primary Education in Cawnpore municipality.
File no. 1195/1927	Compulsory Primary Education in Balrampur municipality.
File no. 568/1928	The progress of education in United Provinces under the reforms.
File no. 1112/1929	Compulsory primary education in Lucknow municipality.
File no. 1055/1930	Compulsory Primary Education in Lakhimpur municipality.
File no. 1025/1933	Resolution by Mrs. Kailash Srivastava regarding girls compulsory education.
File no. 1136/1935	Compulsory primary education for girls in Cawnpore.

File no. 1213/1935	Introduction of Compulsory primary education for girls in Lahanpur Town area, Sitapur.
File no. 1011/1936	Introduction of Compulsory primary education for girls in the Ekdil village of Etawah district.
File no. 927/1936	Girls education at Rai baeralli.
File no. 1063/1936	Girls education in Kakori village at Lko.
File no. 149/1908	Appointment of Mr. E.A Redford to the Indian Education Services.
File no. 221/1908	Appointment of Mr. E.A Jermyn to the Indian Education Services.
File no. 235/1908	Religious Education in the Govt. School.
File no. 705A/1908	Recurring grant of 6lk for Primary Education.
File no. 265/1918	Distribution of the Govt. of India grant for Education.
File no. 4/1915	Govt. of India special grant for female Education.
File no. 301/1915	Govt. High school Etawah.
File no. 4/1923	Lytton Committee report on Indian School.
File no. 285/1925	Misc. Papers.
File no. 543/1926	V.P. Educational reports for 1925-1926.
File no. 1023/1928	Applicability of the U.P., Primary Education act 1916 or U.P. District Board Primary Education act 1926.
File no. 1231/1929	Opening of special classes for teaching in the govt. vernacular schools for girls Fayzabad.
File no. 1287/1929	Addition of para 244 d-a- new one to the Educational Code 1927, Education.
File no. 267/1931	Addition to paras 128 and 129 of the U.P. educational Code 1927 edition.
File no. 343/1931	Amendement to para 341 of the educational Code.
File no. 84/A	Code of rules for grant-in-aid to Anglo-Vernacular Schools for girls.
File no. 148 A	Education Committee.

File no. 199	Application for a special grant to the a Martinier's Girls.
File no. 213A	Quinquennial Review of Education in India, 1892-93 to 1896-97.
File no. 213A/3	Primary Education in the North-Western Provinces and Oudh.
File no. 332A	Female Education.
File no. 332A/3	Female Normal school, Lko.
File no. 332A/5	Model Girls school.
File no. 332A/6	Establishment for the model girls school.
File no. 332A/11	Importance of female education.
File no. 332A/18	Appointment of Miss E.M. West to the Indian educational Services.
File no. 385A	Shimla Educational Conferences.
File no. 410	Colvin School, Lko.
File no. 526	Educational Conferences.
File no. 679A	Appointment of Mr. E.A. Radford to the Indian Education Services.
File no. 739A	Appointment of Mr. H.C. Norman to the Indian Educational Services.
File no. 765	Quinquennial review of the progress of Education in the NWP and Oudh Provinces.
File no. 759	Education of girls with boys in Primary Vernacular School in the NWP and Oudh.
File no.796A	Appointment of Mr. E.A. Jermyn to the Indian educational Services.
File no. 808A	Appointment of Mr. E.A. Richardson to the Indian Educational services.
File no. 835A	Abolition of fees in Primary School.
File no. 853A	Scheme for regarding the Provincial Education Services establishment in the United Provinces.
File no. 866A	Scholarships for the promotion of higher education among women.

File no. 615	Payment of grant to the municipal Boards for compulsory primary education for girls in 1940-41.
File no. 456	Appointment of D.B. Shahjahanpur for female education.
File no. 708	Proposal for raising girls primary school and lower middle standard in the district in the district of Badaun, Meerut, Sitapur, Gorakhpur.
File no. 1233/1927	Opening of 9 additional vernacular schools for girls.
File no. 1141/1932	Opening of 3 govt. schools for girls.
File no. 526/1936	Amendment to the U.P. Educational Code.
File no. 588/1937	Opening of a govt. girls high school at Etawah.
File no. 1108/1931	Compulsory primary Education in the Balrampur (Gonda Dstrict).
File no. 231A/3	Primary education in Oudh.
File no. 317	Tabular forms of the education.
File no. 385A/5	Primary education.
File no. 394A	University Education.
File no. 32	Report on Female infanticide in Oudh for the year 1885-86.
File no. 72/1908	Distribution of district into educational divisions.
File no. 80/1908	Establishment of govt. high schools in United Provinces.
File no. 119/1908	5 lakhs grants for University Education.
File no. 120/1908	Recurring grant of 6 lakhs of Primary Education.
File no. 138/1908	General improvement of Secondary Education.
File no. 190/1908	Rules of the Provincial text- books committee.
File no. 42/1909	Proceeding of the Provincial text-books committee.
File no. 382/1910	Vernacular Education in Schools.
File no. 12/1911	Proceeding of the Provincial text book committee.

File no. 171/1911	Conference of Orientalists held on Shimla in July, 1911.
File no. 198/1911	Proposal to make Elementary education free in all govt., boards, municipal, and aided schools.
File no. 199/1911	Improvement and extension of the system of primary education.
File no. 11/1912	System of grants-in-aid for the primary schools for Indians.
File no. 86/1912	Informal Conference at Shimla to enquire into the question of the education europeans and anglo-indians.
File no. 139/1913	Reorganization of the Inspecting staff for girls schools United Provinces.
File no. 328/1913	Proposal for the appointment of a second Indian education service inspectress for girls schools in the United Provinces.
File no. 454/1913	Concessions to schools mistress and female members of the inspecting staff.
File no. 313/1914	Revision of the district inspecting staff, United Provinces.
File no. 278/1914	Proceedings of the Conference of Inspectors of schools held in June 1914.
File no. 189/1915	Rules for the provincial text-book committee.
File no. 252/1915	Appointment of a committee to consider the curricula for anglo-vernacular and vernacular schools for girls.
File no. 26/1916	Proceeding of the annual general meeting of the text-book committee held on 7 Dec. 1915.
File no. 211/1916	Proceeding of the provincial maktab committee.
File no. 64/1917	Proceeding of the text-book committee.
File no. 195/1917	Education of the children of indigenous dais by the means of scholarships etc.
File no. 213/1917	Staff for the proposed govt. high schools for Indian girls at Lko.

File no. 193/1919	Creation of a post of chief inspector of vernacular education in the United Provinces.
File no.80/1919	Proposal for the appointment of inspectress of training institution in the United Provinces.
File no. 722/1922	Expansion of primary education.
File no. 725/1922	Expansion of vernacular education in district board area.
File no. 324/1923	Lee commission report, recommendation of IES.
File no. 1020/1925	U.P. District Boards Primary Education act, 1926.
File no. 1083/1925	Opening of Hindu Pathshala by district boards and applications for grants for the same.
File no. 1158/1926	Rules by govt. U.P. Primary Education 1926.
File no. 1105/1927	Girls Education.
File no. 1127/1928	D. M. Committee Over Women Education.
File no. 550(37)	Grant to girls education 1941-42.
File no. 422/1942	Compulsory girls education in Cawnpore
File no. 305/1921	Govt. high school at Allahabad.
File no. 213/1926	Female Infanticide, NWP.
File no. 708,	Female Infanticide, NWP

Newspapers

- Abhyudaya Allahabad (1907).
- Aftabhi Punjab
- Bharat Jiwan (Benaras) (1884).
- Bhavishya (Allahabad) 1930 weekly.
- Central Hindu College Magazine (Benaras) 1903, Monthly.
- Chaturvedi (Agra, Lucknow, Kanpur) 1914, Monthly.
- Democract (Allahabad) 1918, weekly, Etd. By Harsh Dev Oli.
- Hindi Pradeep (Allahabad) 1877, monthly.
- Hindustan (Lucknow) Weekly.
- Indian Ladies Magazine (London) monthly.

- Indian magazine and Review (London) monthly.
- Lawrence Gazette, 1871.
- Leader (Allahabad) 1909, Daily, Started by Madan Mohan Malviya.
- National Herald (Lucknow) 1938 , Daily.
- Native Newspaper Reports (United Provinces) up to the name of the provinces was NWP.
- Roshni (Lucknow) 1938 Quarterly, Journal of the All India Women's Conferences.
- Urdu Akhbar, 1877.

Records at Nehru Memorial Library

Hansa Mehta Work

II. Subject files, Installment- I

- File no. 3, Papers concerning establishment of a permanent office for AIWC and articles on the rights and status of women, 1935
- File no.7, Important papers and correspondence of All- Indian Women's Conferences and Draft of Indian Women's Charter of Rights and Duties, 1944-46.
- File no. 8, Draft of the pamphlet on Women's Welfare, 1945.

III. Speeches and Writings by Hansa Mehta.

- File no. 3, Speech on Upliftment of Indian Women, 1940.
- File no. 11, Role of Women in New Indian–Convocation add. In BHU, 1949.
- File no. 20, Education for Women–an Article, 1950-51.
- File no. 68 A Speech on Some Aspects of Women's Education., undated.

Quinquennial Review

- A.M. Nashq, Progress of Education in India 1887-88 to 1891-92 Second Quimquennial Review.
- J.S. Cotton, Progress of Education in India 1892-93 to 1896-97., Third Quinquennial Review.
- R. Nathan , Progress of Education in India, 1897-98 to 1901-02, Fourth Quinquennial Review Vol. II.

- H.W. Orange, Progress of Education in India 1907-12, Sixth Quinquennial Review Vol. II.
- H. Sharp, Progress of Education in India 1912-17, Seventh Quinquennial Review Vol. I and II.
- J.A. Richey, Progress of Education in India 1917-22, Eight Quinquennial Review Vol. I and II.
- R. Littlehailes, Progress of Education in India 1922-27, Ninth Quinquennial Review Vol.I.

Government Published Records

- Census of India- 1921, United Provinces of Agra and Oudh, Vol. XVI, Part-1 Report by E.H.H. Edye, ICS Superintendent , Census Operation Allahabad, Govt. Press, 1923.
- Administration Report of NWP and Oudh of 1895-96, Allahabad.
- Administration Report of United Provinces 1905-06, Allahabad.
- Administration Report of United Provinces 1906-07, Allahabad.
- Administration Report of United Provinces 1904-05, Allahabad, 1906.
- Administration Report of United Provinces Of Agra and Oudh 1933-34, Lucknow 1935 published.
- Administration Report of NWP and Oudh, 1895-96.
- Administration Report of United Provinces 1907-08.
- Administration Report of NWP and Oudh 1887-88.
- Administration Report of NWP and Oudh 1897-98.
- Administration Report of NWP and Oudh 1899-1900, Allahabad printed at NWP and Oudh Press 1901.
- Administration Report of United Provinces of Agra and Oudh 1902-03, Allahabad.
- Administration Report of United Provinces of Agra and Oudh 1904-05, Allahabad, 1906 published.
- Administration Report of United Provinces of Agra and Oudh 1905-06, Allahabad.
- Administration Report of United Provinces of Agra and Oudh 1906-07, Allahabad.

- Administrative Report of United Provinces of Agra and Oudh 1911-12, Allahabad.
- Administration Report of United Provinces of Agra and Oudh 1923-24, Allahabad , 1925
- Administration report of United Provinces of Agra and Oudh 1924-25, Allahabad 1926.
- Administration Report of United Provinces of Agra and Oudh 1925-26 , Lucknow 1927.
- Administration Report of United Provinces of Agra and Oudh 1926-27, Lucknow 1928.
- Administration Report of United Provinces of United Provinces of Agra and Oudh 1927-28, Lucknow, 1929.
- Administration Report of United Provinces of Agra and Oudh 1928-29, Lucknow, 1930 published.
- Administration Report of United Provinces of Agra and Oudh 1929-30, Lucknow, 1931.
- Administration Report of United Provinces of Agra and Oudh 1930-31, Lucknow, 1932.
- Administration Report of United Provinces of Agra and Oudh 1932-33, Allahabad, 1934.
- Administration Report of United Provinces of Agra and Oudh 1931-32, Allahabad, 1933.
- Administration Report of United Provinces of Agra and Oudh 1935-36, Allahabad, 1937.
- Administration Report of United Provinces 1936, Allahabad.
- R.T.H. Griffith, Report on the progress of Education in the NWP and Oudh for the year 1875-76, Officiating Director of Public Instruction, NWP. Allahabad, NWP Govt. Press, 1876.
- M. Kempson, Report on the Progress of Education in the NWP and Oudh for the year 1876-77, M.A., Director of Public Instruction, NWP and Oudh. Allahabad, Press 1877.
- Report on the Public Instruction in the NWP and Oudh for the year 1877-78, Allahabad.
- R.T.H. Griffith , Report on Public Instruction in NWP and Oudh for the year ending 31st March 1880, Allahabad, NWP and Oudh Govt, Press, 1880.

- R. Nathan, Progress of Education in India 1897-98 to 1901-02, Fourth Quinquennial Review, CIE Indian Civil Services, 1904, Calcutta Published.
- John Sargent, Progress of Education in India 1932-1937, M.A., Educational Commissioner with the Govt. of India, 11th Quinquennial Review, Vol.1, Published by the manager of publication, Delhi, 1940.
- J.S. Cotton, Progress of Education in India 1892-93 to 1896-97, Third Quinquennial Review 1898, London, Printed for her majesty's Stationary Office, by Darling and son Ltd, 1-3, Great St. Thomas Apostle, E.C., 1898 Published.
- The Imperial Gazetteer of India Vol. xxiv Oxford, 1908 At the Claredon Press, 1908.
- The Imperial Gazetteer of India, the Indian Empire Vol. IV Administrative, Oxford At the Claredon Press, 1907.
- Statistics of British India for 1910-11 and proceeding years part VII - Educational, Calcutta, Superintendent Govt. Printing India, 1912.
- Department of Statistics India, Statistical Abstract for British India, Vol. V, Education 1913-14, Calcutta Superintendent Govt. Printing India, 1915
- Department of Statistics India, Statistics British India. Vol. V. Education 1914-15, Printing Press India, 1916.
- Department of Statistics India, Statistics of British India, Vol. V Education 1915-16, Calcutta, Superintendent Govt, Printing Press India, 1917.
- 10th issue Department of Statistics India, Statistics of British India, Vol. V Education 1916-17, Calcutta , Superintendent Govt. Printing Press India, 1918.
- Department of Statistics India, Statistics of British India, Vol. V. Education 1917-18, Calcutta, Superintendent Govt. Printing Press India, 1919.
- Department of Statistics India, Statistics of British India, Vol. V Education 1918-19, Calcutta, Superintendent Govt. Printing Press India, 1920.
- Department of Statistics India, Statistics of British India, Vol. V. Education 1919-20, Calcutta, Superintendent Govt. Printing Press India, 1921.

Census

- Census of India, 1911, Vol. I India, Part-I Report by E.A. Gait Fellow of the Royal Satistitical Society, Calcutta, 1913.
- Census of India- 1921, United Provinces of Agra and Oudh, Vol. XVI, Part-1 Report by E.H.H. Edye, ICS Superintendent , Census Operation Allahabad, Govt. Press, 1923.

Secondary Sources Books

- Altekar, A.S., The Position of Women in Hindu Civilization From Prehistoric Times to the Present Day, Motilal Banarsidass Publishers Private Limited, Delhi, 2014.
- A, Mathew. "Christian Missions Education and Nationalism" (From Dominance to compromise) 1870-1930, Anamica Publication, New Delhi. 1999.
- Agrawal, S.P., and Agarwal, J.C., Women's Education In India, Concept Publishing Company, New Delhi, 1992.
- Basu, A. N. Education in Modern India, Orient Book Co., Calcutta, 1947.
- Basu, Arpana, "The Growth of Education and Political Development in India", 1898-1918, Oxford University Press, New Delhi, 1974.
- Basu Aparna, Essays in the History of Indian Education, Concept publishing House, New Delhi, 1982.
- Bellenoit, Hayden J.A., Missionary Education and Empire in Late Colonial India, 1860-1920. London: Pickering & Chatto, 2007.
- Bandyopadhyay, Sekhar, From Plassey to Partition: A History of Modern India, Orient BlackSwan New Delhi, 2013.
- Barton, James.L., Educational Missions, New York, 1913.
- Braisted, Paul Judson, Indian Nationalism and Christian Colleges, Association Press, New York, 1935.
- Bhattacharya Sabyasachi, Bara Joseph, Yagati Chinna Rao, and Sankhdher,(ed.), The Development of Women's Education in India: A Collection of Documents 1850-1920, Kanishka Publishers New Delhi, 2001.

- Bhattacharya Sabyasachi, Bara Joseph, Yagati Chinna Rao, Educating the Nation Documents on the Discourse of National Education in India, 1880-1920, Kanishka Publishers, New Delhi, 2003.
- Bhattacharya Sabyasachi, Education and the Disprivileged Nineteenth and twentieth century India, Orient Longman, New Delhi, 2002.
- Caton, A.R., The Key Of Progress: A Survey of the Status and Conditions of Women in India, London, 1930.
- Carpenter, M., Six Months in India, London, 1868.
- Chanana Karuna, Transformation Links between Higher and Basic Education Mapping the Field, Sage Publication, New Delhi, 2004.
- Chandra, Bipin, Nationalism and Colonialism in Modern India ,Orient Longman Ltd., Delhi, 1979.
- Chapman, P., Hindu Female Education, London, 1839.
- Cousins, M.E., Indian Womanhood Today, Allahabad, 1941.
- Cousins, M.E., The Awakening of Asian Womanhood, Ganesh and Co. Madras, 1922.
- Cowan, Minna G., The Education of the Women of India -Primary Source Edition, Fleming H. Revell Co. New York, 1912.
- Dayal, Bhagwan. The Development of Modern Indian Education, Orient Longmans Ltd. Bombay, 1955.
- Das, S., Purdah The Status of Indian Women, Ess Ess Publication, New Delhi, 1979.
- Das, S.K., The Educational System of Ancient Hindu, Calcutta, 1930.
- D, Basu, B., History of Education in India, Under The Rule of The East India Company, Hard Press Publishing, no date mention.
- Desai, Tripta, Women in India, Munshiram Manoharlal Publishers Pvt. Ltd., 1992.
- Desai and Krishnaraj, Women and Society in India, New Delhi, Ajanta Publications, 1990.
- Desai, Neera and Krishna Raj, Maitreyi, Women and Society in India, New Delhi, Ajantha Publications, 1987.

- Etherington, Norman, ed. Missions and Empire. Oxford: Oxford University Press, 2005.
- Forbes, Geraldine, Women in Modern India, Cambridge University Press, 2012.
- Forbes, Geraldine, Women in Colonial India, Chronicles Books, New Delhi, 2005.
- Farquhar, J.N., Modern Religious Movements in India, Macmillan & Co., London, 1913.
- Geetha, V., Patriarchy, Published by Stree, Kolkata, 2015.
- Geetha, V., Gender, Published by Stree, Kolkata, 2012.
- Gandhi, Leela, Postcolonial Theory, Oxford University Press, New Delhi, 2015.
- Gandhi, M.K., Women and Social Injustice, Navjivan Publishing House Ahmedabad, 1958.
- Gandhi, M.K., Christian Missions: Their Place in India: Collection of Articles and Utterances on Christian Missions, Navajivan Publishing House, Ahmedabad, 1941.
- Ghosh, Suresh Chandra, The History of Education in Modern India 1757-2012, Orient Black Swan, New Delhi, 2013.
- Ghosh, Suresh Chandra, Birth of A New India, Originals, Delhi, 2001.
- Gokhale, G.K., Speech on The Elementary Education Bill, Poona Printed at the Arya Bushan Press, 1911.
- Goodall, Norman, A History of the London Missionary Society, 1895-1945, Oxford University Press, London, 1954.
- Gragg, Kenneth, Christianity in World Perspective, Lutterworth Press, London, 1968.
- Gupta, Charu, Gendering Colonial India Reforms, Print, Caste and Communalism, Orient Blackswan, New Delhi, 2012.
- Gupta, Nirmala, Educational Development–A Historical Development, Anamika Publishers Ltd. New Delhi, 1999.
- Gupta, N.L., Women Education Through The Ages, Concept Publishing Company, New Delhi, 2000.
- Goswami, Sambrodh, Female Infanticide and Child Marriage, Rawat Publication, New Delhi, 2007.

- Hartog, Sir Philip. Some Aspects of Indian Education: Present and Past, Oxford University Press, London, 1939.
- Hauswrith, Frieda, Purdah The Status of Indian Women, London, 1932.
- Ingham, Kenneth, Reformers in India 1793-1833 An Account of the Work of Christian Missionarires on Behalf of Social Reform, Cambridge, 1956.
- Jain, Devaki (ed), Indian Women, Publication Division of Ministry of Information and Broadcasting, Government of India, 1996.
- James, H.R., Education and Statesmanship in India, Longmans, Green & Co. London, 1917
- Keay, F. E., A History of Education in India and Pakistan, Oxford University Press, 1959.
- Kapoor, A.N., The Gandhian Era, Radha Publication, New Delhi, 2007.
- Kapur , Promilla, Empowering The Indian Woman, Publications Division, New Delhi, 2001.
- Kumar, Krishna & Oesterheld, Joachim. Education and Social Change in South Asia. Orient Longman Private Limited, New Delhi. 1996.
- Kumar, Krishna, Political Agenda of Education, Second Edition, Sage Publication, New Delhi, 2005.
- Kumar, Radha, The History of Doing, Zubaan Publishers, New Delhi, 1993.
- Kumar, Nita, The Politics of Gender, Community and Modernity Essays on Education in India, Oxford Press, New Delhi, 2007.
- Mayhew, Arthur. Christianity and the Government of India. London: Faber & Gwyer Ltd., 1929.
- Mayhew Arthur, The Education of India, London, 1926.
- McCully, Bruce T., English Education and the Origins of Indian Nationalism. Columbia University Press, New York, 1940.
- Menon, Neveditha (ed), Themes in Politics. Gender and Politics in India, New Delhi, Oxford University Press, 1999.

- Mathur, Y.B., Women's Education in India 1813-1966, Asia Publishing House, Bombay, 1973.
- Martin, Jane and Goodman, Joyce, Women and Education, 1800-1980, Palgrave Macmillan, 2004.
- Mudaliar, A. Lakshmanaswami, Education in India. Asia Publication House, New Delhi, 1960.
- Mukherjee, S.N. History of Education in India, Acharya Book Depot, Baroda, 1951.
- Narayan, Manish, Educational Thoughts of Bal Gangadhar Tilak, Mukund Publication, Delhi, 2009.
- Naidu, Sarojini, Speeches and Writings, 3rd edition, G.A.Nateson, Madras, 1904.
- Nehru, Jawaharlal, Women of India, The Publication Division New Delhi , 1958.
- Nirmal, Chiranjivi, J., Human Rights in India, Historical, Social, and Political Perspective, Oxford University Press, 2009.
- Nurullah, S. and J.P. Niak, A History of Education in India. Macmillan & Co. Ltd., London, 1951.
- Philips, C.H. The East India Company, 1784-1838. Manchester University Press, Manchester, 1940.
- Panigrahi Lalitha, British Social policy and Female Infanticide in India, Munshiram Manoharlal, New Delhi, 1972.
- Paranjpe, M.R., ed., A Source Book on Modern Indian Education, Macmillan Bombay, 1938.
- Khullar Mala, ed., Writing the Women's Movement A Reader, Kali Publisher, New Delhi, Published 2005, Reprinted 2006.
- Kumar Deepak, Bara Joseph, Khadria Nandita, Gayatri Radha, (ed), Education In Colonial India Historical Insights, Manohar Publication, New Delhi, 2013.
- Kumar, Krishna, Politics of Education in Colonial India, (second edition), Sage Publication, New Delhi, 2005.
- Rawat, P.N. History of Indian Education. Bharat Publications, Agra, 1956.

- Rao , Parimala V., ed., New Perspective in the History of Indian Education, Orient Black Swan, New Delhi, 2014.
- Roy, Ram Mohan, The Renaissance of Hinduism ,Hindu University Press, Benares, 1944.
- Richter, Julius A., A History of Missions in India, Oliphant, Anderson & Frrier, London, 1908.
- Satthianadhan, S., History of Education in the Madras Presidency, Srinivasa Varadhachari & Co., Madras, 1894.
- Sangari, Kumkum and Vaid Sudesh, (ed.), Recasting Women Essays in Colonial India, Zubaan Publication, New Delhi, 1989.
- Sarkar, Tanika, Hindu Wife, Hindu Nation, Community, Religion and Cultural Nationalism, Permanent Black, New Delhi 2001, fourth Impression 2011.
- Sankhadher, B.M., Encyclopedia of Education System in India, Deep and Deep Publications Ltd. No date.
- Shabbir, S., History of Educational Development in Vidarbha from 1882 to 1923 A.D., Northern Book Centre, New Delhi, 2005.
- Sen, Indrani, Memsahib's Writings Colonial Narratives on Indian Women, Orient Black Swan, 2008.
- Serto , Manilei, Women Education and Development, Maxford Books, New Delhi, 2011.
- Singh, Arvind Kumar, The Builder of Modern India, Gurukul Publishers, Delhi, 2009.
- Siqueria, T.N., The Education of India: History and Problems, Oxford University Press, London.
- Sreenivas, Mytheli, Wives, Widows and Concubines the Conjugal Family Ideal in Colonial India, Orient Blackswan, New Delhi, 2009.
- Shridevi, S., A Century of Indian Womanhood, Rao and Raghavan, Mysore, 1965.
- Sudha, D. K., Gender Role, New Delhi, APH Publications, 2000.
- Trevelyan, C.E., On the Education of the People of India. Longman Orme, Brown, Greene & Longmans, London, 1838.
- Thomas, F.W., The History and Prospects of British Education in India, Cambridge, 1981.

- Vakil, K.S., Education in India, T.C.E. Journals & Publications, Lucknow, 1948.
- Vyas, K. C. The Development of National Education in India, Vora & Co., Publishers Ltd.

E-Source Journals/Articles

- Shodhganga. Inflibnet.ac.in.
- Anderson Fix Nancy, Bridging Cross Cultural Feminisim: Annie Beasent and Women's Right in England and India, 1874- 1933, Women's History Review, 314, 563-580, DOI; 10.1080/ 09612029400200070, accessed on 24-03- 2016.
- Malavika Kasturi, Female Infanticide; Selections from the Records of the Government of the North-Western Provinces, Second Series, Volume VIII, Allahabad, 1871, Indian Journal of Gender Studies, 7:1 (2000).
- L.S., Vishwanathan, (Discussion) Female Infanticide, Economic and Politically Weekly, September1, 2001.
- L.S., Vishwanath, Efforts of Colonial State to Suppress Female Infanticide: Use of Sacred Texts, Generation of Knowledge, Economic and political Weekly. 33 (19) May 9, 1998.P.1104-1112.
- P.K. Srivastava, Female Infanticide in 19th Century India: A Genocide? Advances in Historical Studies, 3, 269-284, http:// dx.doi.org/10.4236/ahs.2014.35022.
- Asha Basumatary, Study of Institution of Female Infanticide in Colonial India, Journal of International Academic Research For Multidisciplinary, ISSN: 2320-5083, Volume 3, Issue 7, August 2015.
- Madhu Kishwar, Arya Samaj and Women's Education: Kanya Mahavidyalaya, Jalandhar, Economic Political Weekly, Vol. 21, No. 17 (Apr. 26, 1986), pp. WS9-WS13+WS15-WS 24., http:// www.jstor.org/stable/4375593 , accessed on 11.09.2014.
- George Allen Odgers, Education in British India, The Phi Delta Kappan, Vol. 8, No. 2 (Oct., 1925), pp. 1-6 Published, accessed on 11.09.2014.
- S. Shridevi, Women's Higher Education in India since Independence, Improving College and University Teaching, Vol. 20, No. 1, The

Higher Education of Women (Winter, 1972), pp. 71-72, published by: Taylor & Francis, Ltd., accessed on 11.09.2014.

- James Digges La Touche, The United Provinces of Agra and Oudh, Journal of the Royal Society of Arts, Vol. 56, No. 2900 (June 19, 1908), pp. 756-769, Published by: Royal Society for the Encouragement of Arts, Manufactures and Commerce, accessed on 26.09.2014.
- Lady Hartog, The Education of Girls in India, Journal of the Royal Society of Arts, Vol. 84, No. 4348 (MARCH 20th, 1936), pp. 499-517 Published by: Royal Society for the Encouragement of Arts, Manufactures and Commerce, accessed on 11.09.2014.
- Syama Prasad Mookerjee, Education in British India, Annals of the American Academy of Political and Social Science, Vol. 233, India Speaking (May, 1944), pp. 30-38, Sage Publications, Inc, accessed on 11.09.2014.
- Lata Mani, Contentious Traditions: The Debate on Sati in Colonial India, Cultural Critique, No. 7, The Nature and Context of Minority Discourse II (Autumn,1987), pp. 119-156 , Published by: University of Minnesota Press, accessed on 11.09.2014.
- James Johnston, Education in India and the India Commission on Education, Journal of the Statistical Society of London, Vol. 46, No. 2 (Jun., 1883), pp. 225-282 ,Published by: Wiley for the Royal Statistical Society, accessed on 26.09.2014.
- Sophie M. Tharakan and Michael Tharakan, Status of Women in India: A Historical Perspective, Social Scientist, Vol. 4, No. 4/5, Special Number on Women (Nov. - Dec., 1975), pp.115-123, Published by: Social Scientist, accessed on 11.09.2014.
- A.R. Kamat, Women's Education and Social Change in India, Social Scientist, Vol. 5, No. 1 (Aug., 1976), pp. 3-27 ,Published by: Social Scientist, accessed on 11.09.2014.
- Padma Anagol, The Emergence of the Female Criminal in India: Infanticide and Survival under the Raj History ,Workshop Journal, No. 53 (Spring, 2002), pp. 73-93, Published by: Oxford University Press, accessed on 11.09.2014.
- M.S. Sundaram, A Century of British Education in India 1857-1957, Journal of the Royal Society of Arts, Vol. 107, No. 5035 (June 1959),

pp. 491-507, Published by: Royal Society for the Encouragement of Arts, Manufactures and Commerce, accessed on 11.09.2014.

- Mary Carpenter, On Female Education in India, Bristol Selected Pamphlets, (1868) Published by: University of Bristol Library, accessed on 26.09.2014.
- Geraldine H. Forbes, In Search of the 'Pure Heathen': Missionary Women in Nineteenth Century India, Economic and Political Weekly, Vol. 21, No. 17 (Apr. 26, 1986), pp. WS2-WS8, accessed on 20.10.2013.

Unpublished Ph.D Thesis/Dessertations

- Shakkela.U.V., Perception of Women's Emancipation in Nineteenth Century India, Dessertation Submitted in Department of History, Pondicherry University, 2003.
- Menon, Sujata, Women Education: Their Role in Society in British Gujarat: 1850-1947, Dessertation Submitted in Department of History, to The Maharaja Sayajirao University of Baroda, 2007.
- Taneja Anup, Women in the National Movement For India's Independence: 1920-1947, Thesis Submitted in Department of History, to Bundelkhand University, 2002.
- Savita, Women's Education in Bihar: 1890-1950, Thesis Submitted in Department of Centre Of Historical Studies School Of Social Sciences, Jawaharlal Nehru University, 2006.
- Mohammad Dilshad Mohabbat, Development of Education in the Colonial Punjab: The Role of Christian Missionaries (1847-1947), Thesis Submitted in Department Of History to University of The Punjab, Lahore.
- Joy Evans, Women's Cultural Agency in British India: Challenging Indian Culture with Female Education, Thesis Submitted in Department of History, Vanderbilt University, 2001.

Index